New Life

Growing in the new life that's only possible in Jesus Christ

TABLE OF CONTENTS

OVERVIEW OF NEW LIFE

New Life Purpose

New Life is a discipleship resource that's driven by Scripture and focused on making disciples of Jesus Christ who are equipped to live on mission to make disciples. New Life is a resource for discipleship groups in the church, and the material is designed for utilization in small, gender-specific discipleship groups of 3-5 people.

New Life Approach

Jesus said that "everyone who practices sin is a slave to sin" (John 8:34). This problem isn't limited to only a few, but it's *the* problem of every person ever born into the world. "All have sinned and fall short of the glory of God," and "the wages of sin is death" (Romans 3:23 & 6:23a). Every person in the world is born into sin, and each person – in varying ways – quickly becomes enslaved to sin. As a result of these biblical truths, New Life recognizes that this spiritual condition can only be conquered by the saving power of God through the gospel of Jesus Christ (Romans 1:16, 6:23b, 5:8, 8:1-2, 10:9, etc.).

The gospel is the good news that although all of us are sinners, God has made a way for forgiveness and victory over sin through his Son, Jesus Christ. The gospel is the message of the sinless life of Jesus; the sacrificial death of Jesus for our sin; and the burial and resurrection of Jesus that brought victory over sin and death. This message is the power of God unto salvation for all who believe, and it is the message that confirms the new life that's possible by God's grace through repentance and faith in Jesus Christ (Romans 6:1-14).

New Life is based on the truth that the gospel is the only hope for those who are enslaved to sin and that the gospel is the only hope for transformation in a life that's been set free in Christ Jesus. There are no steps or processes that can replace the power of the Holy Spirit through the message of the gospel in the life of the one who believes. As a result, New Life focuses on the good news of the gospel that has the power to set someone free from slavery to sin (Galatians 5:1). Through the gospel, God made the way to give us a relationship with him and life with him. Through the gospel, God made the way for us to grow in our new life in Christ, changing us to desire his way over our way and transforming our thoughts by his truth (Galatians 2:20; Romans 12:1-2). This is the work of God through the gospel of Jesus Christ. It's the work of God in saving us by his grace through faith in Jesus, and it's the work of God in transforming us in his grace to look more-and-more like Jesus.

New Life is focused on an intense study of Ephesians 4 and 5, in a format that encourages believers to understand what God's Word means and to apply God's Word to their lives. The goal is growth in the Lord, taking off the old life and putting on the new life that's only possible in Jesus Christ.

New Life Format

Weekly discipleship groups are divided by gender, and the focus of the weekly group is to provide a place where group members can worship the Lord together, praying for one another and looking to God's Word for new life in Christ. The hope is that New Life discipleship groups would be a place where members can openly share their testimonies about the struggles and successes of the past week and can have gospel truth from God's Word applied to their lives. The format of the New Life material in a discipleship group includes the following 2-week break-down of each lesson.

Week 1
(1) Fellowship and prayer
(2) Bible reading plan follow-up
(3) New Life lesson intro
    (a) Lesson overview
    (b) "Hearing God's Word"
    (c) "Applying God's Word"

Week 2
(1) Fellowship and prayer
(2) Bible reading plan follow-up
(3) New Life lesson progress
    (a) "Responding to God's Word"
    (b) "Living God's Word"
    (c) "Praying God's Word"

The purpose of New Life is to proclaim the gospel and to apply the gospel. On a weekly basis, the gospel lesson in New Life will provide clear hope and direction for living in the grace and victory of Christ. Each week, the importance of the church and the ongoing ministry of the Word in the life of a believer will be emphasized and encouraged. Groups are encouraged to use the New Life New Testament reading plan for daily Bible reading and to spend time each meeting sharing with one another about what God is doing in their lives through his Word.

The 26 gospel lessons provided in New Life come from the following passage, which relates to the new life that's possible in Jesus Christ: Ephesians 4:17-5:21. This passage emphasizes the reality of the new life that's given to a believer, and it gives specific instruction to the believer on how to put off their old life of sin and to put on their new life in Christ. Each week, participants will learn from God's Word about what's possible in the new life that's only possible through Christ. Participants will be reminded that new life is possible through God's grace in the life of a believer, and participants will be encouraged to believe and to walk by faith in what the Lord calls them to do through his Word.

New Life Lessons

New Life lessons are short and concise, emphasizing a single truth from God's Word and applying that truth to the life of the participants. The lessons will have a very specific application, always centered on the gospel and the necessary pattern of repentance and faith that's needed to grow in the new life that's given in Jesus.

Below is a summary of the New Life curriculum. There are 26 lessons, which allows the New Life curriculum to be covered in 6 months, or the lessons may be spread out over 2-weeks, allowing for the curriculum to extend to 12 months. For discipleship groups, it's recommended that the 2-week format be used in conjunction with a Bible reading plan.

Here are the titles and Scripture references for the 26 New Life lessons:
(1) The Problem: Sin (Hard hearts separated from God; Ephesians (Eph.) 4:17-19);
(2) The Truth: The Gospel (Eph. 4:20-21; Romans 3:23, 6:23, 5:8, & 10:9);
(3) The Hope: New Life (Renewed minds for living for God; Eph. 4:22-24);
(4) The Old Life (Sinful thoughts, desires, and actions; Eph. 4:17-22);
(5) The New Life ("NL" - Renewed thoughts, desires, and actions; Eph. 4:23-24);
(6) NL: Speak Truth (Identifying lies, confessing lies, speaking truth; Eph. 4:25);
(7) NL: Address Anger (Identify and address anger to avoid sin; Eph. 4:26-27);
(8) NL: Work & Share (Confessing theft, committing to work and share; Eph. 4:28);
(9) NL: Healthy Talk (Identifying corrupting talk, speaking to build up; Eph. 4:29);
(10) NL: Pleasing God (Grieving the Holy Spirit and your redemption; Eph. 4:30);
(11) NL: Sinful Attitudes (Identify and confess; Eph. 4:31);
(12) NL: Godly Attitudes (Identify and request; Eph. 4:32);
(13) NL: Kindness (How, and who? Eph. 4:32);
(14) NL: Forgiveness (Who, and when? Eph. 4:32);
(15) NL: Love (God's love for us, and our love for others; Eph. 5:1-2);
(16) NL: Purity (In the way we live; Eph. 5:3);
(17) NL: Purity in Speech (In the way we speak; Eph. 5:4);
(18) NL: Protection from Deception (Identifying deception, listing partners; Eph. 5:5-8);
(19) NL: Hope in Inheritance (Identifying your identity and inheritance; Eph. 5:5-8);
(20) NL: Exposing Sin (Shining light on sinful actions and repentance; Eph. 5:11-14);
(21) NL: Exposing Sin (Living in the light of Christ; Eph. 5:11-14);
(22) NL: Walking Wisely (Identifying wise and unwise; Eph. 5:15-16);
(23) NL: God's Will (Knowing God's Will for your life; Eph. 5:17);
(24) NL: Living Sober (Filling your life with the Spirit; Eph. 5:18);
(25) NL: Living in a Community of Faith (Discipleship and worship; Eph. 5:19-20); and
(26) NL: Living for Christ (Relationship to others in Christ; Eph. 5:21).

LESSON 1

THE PROBLEM: SIN

Now this I say and testify in the Lord, that you must no longer walk as the Gentiles do, in the futility of their minds. They are darkened in their understanding, alienated from the life of God because of the ignorance that is in them, due to their hardness of heart. They have become callous and have given themselves up to sensuality, greedy to practice every kind of impurity.
Ephesians 4:17-19 (ESV)

"What's your problem?" We've all probably said these words to someone, and we've all probably had someone say these words to us. It happens when we're confronted with sinful attitudes in the behavior of others, and their words and actions hurt us. It happens when our sinful attitudes result in behavior that hurts others. This common question reveals a problem that we all have in our lives. It's actually the biggest problem that everyone faces. It's the problem that knows no boundaries and extends to every race, every nation, every language, and every economic and social group. It's the problem of sin. It's the problem that affects us all because "all have sinned and fall short of the glory of God" (Romans 3:23). It's the problem that enslaves us all! As Jesus said, "Everyone who practices sin is a slave to sin" (John 8:34).

So if sin is the biggest problem facing the world, what's the solution to sin? How can someone be set free from slavery to sin? God provides the answer in his Word, and the answer is the gospel of his Son, Jesus Christ. God made the way for forgiveness and victory over sin through Jesus. The gospel – or good news – is the message of the sinless life of Jesus; the sacrificial death of Jesus for our sin; and the burial and resurrection of Jesus that brought victory over sin and death. This message is the power of God unto salvation for all who believe, and this message is the key to understanding the new life through Christ that's needed to set someone free from sin.

In his letter to the church in Ephesus, the Apostle Paul was concerned about sin. He knew that everyone had this problem, and he also knew that those who had repented of their sin and trusted in the death, burial, and resurrection of Jesus Christ had been set free from sin. However, Paul also knew that while new life had been given, there was much that the believers needed to do to take off their old life of sin and to put on their new life in Jesus. These believers needed to be reminded about their life before Christ, which marks all of our lives without Christ.

Being set free from slavery to sin requires being given new life and then living in the power of that new life, both of which are done only by God's grace in Christ. Here are two important questions for you to answer: Do you have new life in Jesus? Are you living in the power of that new life? Use the worksheet that follows to prayerfully answer these questions in your life.

What does life before Christ look like?

Use the Scripture above to fill in the blanks, and then talk about what each of these things means. How have you experienced these things in your life?

- _____ of their minds;

- _____ in their understanding;

- _____ from the life of God;

- _____ that is in them;

- _____ of heart;

- They have become _____;

- Given themselves up to _____; and

- Greedy to practice every kind of _____.

When someone has new life in Jesus, what can he/she do when it comes to these things?

- You must ____ _____ walk . . . .

It's impossible to do this if you are still enslaved to sin. Read Ephesians 2:1-3. Someone who is dead can't do anything! The only way to live for God is to be born again – given new life – through the Son of God who loved you and died for you. For those who repent and believe in Jesus, their sins are forgiven. They are new creations in Christ, and they are set free from slavery to sin, so that through their new life in Jesus Christ, they can now live for God!

APPLYING GOD'S WORD

Look through the list above related to life apart from Jesus, and answer these questions.

Do you see any of these things in your life? If so, how?

Do these things still define who you are? If so, why?

RESPONDING TO GOD'S WORD

Take time to honestly respond to God's Word about the old life of sin and the new life in Jesus.

Where do you stand with the Lord? Ask the Lord to give you the eyes to see.

Based on the evidence of your life, do you have new life in Christ, or does the evidence of your life say that you are still enslaved to sin and need to be set free by God's grace through Jesus Christ?

LIVING GOD'S WORD

You must no longer walk . . . .

What sin do you need to turn away (repent) from this week?

Share, and pray for one another.

PRAYING GOD'S WORD

Using Ephesians 4:17-19, let the prayer below guide you to look to the Lord for what only he can do in bringing new life in Christ into your life. If you have new life in Jesus, pray that the Lord will grow the new life in you, helping you to take off the old and put on the new!

Lord, help me to no longer walk as those who don't believe and worship you. Give me a new mind that's no longer futile in the way that I think and the things that I think about. Bring the light of your truth into my life. Overcome the darkness that keeps me from understanding. God, my sin has alienated me from your life. I've acted in ignorance, and my heart has been hard towards you. Give me a new heart. I want to be reconciled to you through your Son Jesus, who is my Lord and my Savior. Lord, change me! Make me tenderhearted and not callous. Make me love righteousness and not sin. Lord, I want the new life in Christ that's only possible by your grace. Through Jesus Christ I pray. Amen.

If through this prayer God has brought you new life in Christ, then share that good news with a Christian brother or sister.

LESSON 2

THE TRUTH: THE GOSPEL

But that is not the way you learned Christ! –
assuming that you have heard about him and were taught in him, as the truth is in Jesus.
Ephesians 4:20-21 (ESV)

Let's review the problem we all have, which we focused on in Lesson 1. That problem is sin. Remember, it's the problem that affects us all because "all have sinned and fall short of the glory of God" (Romans 3:23). It's the most significant problem we'll ever have because the wages of sin – what we earn for our sin – is death (Romans 6:23). In other words, we've all broken God's law, and as a result of being found guilty of breaking God's law, we've been sentenced to death. This death is not only physical, but it's spiritual. We're alienated from God (Ephesians 4:18), and we're considered sons of disobedience and children of wrath (Ephesians 2:2-3). This is the reality of who we are as sinners, and the death sentence we receive is eternal! It's an eternal – never ending – death in a place called hell. This is what we deserve for our sin; however, in God's goodness and mercy, he made a way to provide us with what we don't deserve: Forgiveness and new life!

In Romans 6:23, God's truth reveals his grace towards us through Jesus: "For the wages of sin is death, but the free gift of God is eternal life in Christ Jesus our Lord." We've earned death because we're guilty of sinning against God, but he has a free gift that's available to us, which is eternal life in Christ Jesus our Lord. Think about it! The new and eternal life that's possible through Jesus is something that we can't earn or pay for because it's a free gift. It's something that only God can give, and like any gift, once the gift is opened, it belongs to the one who received the gift.

Why would God offer such a gift? How could he offer such a gift? Romans 5:8 helps us answer these questions: "But God shows his love for us in that while we were still sinners, Christ died for us." Why would God offer such a gift to guilty sinners? He offers it because of his great love for us. How could he offer such a gift? If a judge let a convicted murderer go free without any payment or penalty, we'd say that judge was unjust. God can't forget our sins and let us go free if there's no payment or penalty for our sin. That would be unjust, and he is the perfect and just Judge. So how could he offer such a gift? The answer is that he can offer this gift of forgiveness and life because he was willing to give the life of his Son to pay the penalty for our sin. Jesus died for our sin, and on the third day, the Father raised him from the dead, defeating sin and death for us all.

Incredibly, God invites us to respond to this message of Jesus (the gospel) by repenting of sin (turning away from) and confessing our faith in Jesus Christ as our Savior and Lord (Romans 10:9). Have you responded to the gospel? This is the starting place for new life!

8

What are some of the things that are necessary for new life in Christ?

Use the Scripture above to fill in the blanks, and then talk about what each of these things means.

- **But that is not the way you _____ Christ!**

- **Assuming that you have _____ about him**

- **And were _____ in him,**

- **As the _____ is in Jesus.**

What do these verses emphasize about what's needed to know and to grow in a new life in Christ?

APPLYING GOD'S WORD

Look through the list above, and answer these questions.

Are any of these things a reality in your life? When, and how?

Which of these things are still important in your life today? Why?

RESPONDING TO GOD'S WORD

Take time to honestly respond to God's Word about the truth that's in Jesus.

How do you need to respond to hearing and to learning about the gospel of Jesus Christ today?

Do you want the truth in your life? Where is the truth found? Ask the Lord to help you focus on Jesus Christ in your life for all you need to find the truth.

LIVING GOD'S WORD

Learned . . . heard . . . taught . . .

Go to church and to a small group Bible study to learn about God's Word this week.

When you would normally listen to music this week, listen to God's Word to hear his truth in your life.

Be teachable! Ask the Lord to help you accept the truth that you hear and learn from his Word.

PRAYING GOD'S WORD

Using Ephesians 4:20-21, let the prayer below guide you to look to the Lord in your life. If you have new life in Jesus, pray that the Lord will ground you in the new life you have, and if you need new life in Jesus, pray that the Lord will teach you and lead you to the truth.

Lord, I praise you for your love for me that you proved by sending your Son Jesus to die for my sin. I confess to you that I don't always live in the way that I learned in Christ. I want to learn more about Jesus, and I want to live more like Jesus. O God, from what I've heard about Jesus, please help me to understand the truth. Give me a teacher and preacher who will help me hear your Word and who will teach me and help me learn about Jesus. I believe that the truth is in Jesus. Help me to see, to understand, and to believe the truth! I pray all of this through Jesus Christ, your Son and my Savior. Amen.

LESSON 3

THE HOPE: NEW LIFE

To put off your old self, which belongs to your former manner of life and is corrupt through deceitful desires, and to be renewed in the spirit of your minds, and to put on the new self, created after the likeness of God in true righteousness and holiness.
Ephesians 4:22-24 (ESV)

One essential for living for God in our lives and for growing in the new life that God gives us in Christ is a renewed mind. In order to put off the old self, we need to be made new! We need a new way of thinking and a new way of seeing things in order to break away from our former manner of life that's corrupt through deceitful desires. Isn't that true? Haven't you experienced this in your life?

Satan is the father of lies (John 8:44), and he seeks to kill, steal, and destroy (John 10:10). Our old self – enslaved to sin – is the proof of these realities. The world is full of Satan's lies. Just sleep with this person or that person . . . you'll feel so good and will feel so much better about yourself. Just drink another drink or take another pill . . . you'll be the fun and exciting person you always wanted to be, or you'll be able to escape to a place where you don't have so many problems and worries. Just stay another hour . . . this business can't make it without you, and there's no way you're gonna let someone else look like they work harder than you do. Just look at a little more porn . . . it'll give you satisfaction, and who's it going to hurt? We could go on-and-on, couldn't we? Do these things ever deliver what they promise? Perhaps there's a glimpse of delivering on the promise, but it's fleeting. It never lasts long. What can we count on for all of these things? They will kill, steal, and destroy. That's what sin does. Little-by-little or sometimes all at once like a landslide, sin kills us on the inside, and it kills healthy relationships with others. It steals the promises of reward that we thought it would bring. It destroys our lives and often the lives of those we most love. This is what deceitful desires do, but how do we conquer those desires? We conquer them by God's grace through the renewing of our minds in Christ Jesus.

The new self or new life isn't about recovering our old sinful self – our former manner of life. The new life is about God redeeming us and sanctifying us by his power through the work of Christ in the gospel. The death and resurrection of Jesus is our victory! His death for our sins and his resurrection bring us new life, which is being created in the likeness of God. This is your pursuit and God's desire for your life: That you would look more like him!

Putting on your new self in Christ requires the renewal of the spirit of your minds through the unchanging Word of God. Putting on your new self looks like desires and attitudes and actions that look more like God, growing in true righteousness and holiness. This is something that only God can do; and nothing is impossible with God!

HEARING GOD'S WORD

What does the new life look like?

Use the Scripture above to fill in the blanks, and then talk about what each of these things means.

- **To _____ _____ your old self;**

- **Which belongs to your _____ manner of life;**

- **And is corrupt through _____ desires;**

- **Be _____ in the spirit of your minds;**

- **To _____ _____ the new self;**

- **Created after the _____ of God;**

- **In true _____ and _____.**

APPLYING GOD'S WORD

Look through the list above, and answer these questions.

What are the defining characteristics of your old self (maybe who you are now)?

What would these things look like in the new self described in Ephesians 4:22-24?

RESPONDING TO GOD'S WORD

Take time to honestly respond to God's Word about the old self and the new self.

What do you need to do to put off the old self? Do you need to take the first step of repentance and faith in Jesus? How do you need to apply the gospel to help you take a step of obedience in your life right now?

What do you need to do to put on the new self? Do you need to take the first step of repentance and faith in Jesus? How do you need to apply the gospel to help you take a step of obedience in your life right now?

LIVING GOD'S WORD

Put on the new self . . . .

Read God's Word every day to start filling your mind with his truth and allowing the Holy Spirit to renew your mind.

What would it look like to look more like God this week?

PRAYING GOD'S WORD

Using Ephesians 4:22-24, let the prayer below guide you to look to the Lord for what only he can do in growing new life in Christ into your life. If you have new life in Jesus, pray that the Lord will grow the new life in you, helping you to take off the old and put on the new!

Lord, I worship you because you are the giver of life and the only one with the power to give new life. Help me to put off my old self. I don't want to live in my former manner of life, doing the same things, feeling the same way, and experiencing the same results. Set me free from the things that corrupt and from being driven by deceitful desires. I confess that I desire things that I shouldn't at times, and I praise you for reminding me that these desires are deceitful, promising something good but always leading to something bad. Father, renew me in the spirit of my mind, and give me the power in Christ to put on the new self, created after the likeness of God in true righteousness and holiness. Grow a desire in my heart to look more like you! Help me to grow in holiness to stamp out sinfulness in my life. I ask these things through your Son Jesus. Amen.

LESSON 4

THE OLD LIFE

Now this I say and testify in the Lord, that you must no longer walk as the Gentiles do, in the futility of their minds. They are darkened in their understanding, alienated from the life of God because of the ignorance that is in them, due to their hardness of heart. They have become callous and have given themselves up to sensuality, greedy to practice every kind of impurity. But that is not the way you learned Christ!—assuming that you have heard about him and were taught in him, as the truth is in Jesus, to put off your old self, which belongs to your former manner of life and is corrupt through deceitful desires.
Ephesians 4:17-22 (ESV)

The old self or old life is our life before Christ. For every single one of us, that life is defined by sinful thoughts, desires, and actions. The apostle Paul's life before Christ was defined by sinful thoughts, desires, and actions. He was a religious leader among the Jewish people. He was incredibly passionate about protecting the Jewish faith and following God's commandments as he understood them. However, his thoughts, desires, and actions were sinful. He became a leader in the effort to stamp out Christianity. He stood by in approval as Stephen was stoned to death for his faith and testimony for Jesus (Acts 7:58). He went on a crusade to arrest and to persecute anyone who said that Jesus was the Messiah (Acts 8:1-3). Read Paul's testimony about his life before Christ in Philippians 3:3-7, and you'll see that he realized that all of those things were worthless compared to what he received in Jesus Christ!

What's your testimony of life before Christ? Maybe that's still your life right now today? You need to be able to make a list of what identified you and what you valued in your old life. Perhaps it was like Paul's list. On the surface, some in the world may have considered what you valued in your life as good, but the results have left you and others hurt and empty. Perhaps unlike Paul's list, your list may include serious drug and alcohol use that led to a life that was full of lies and pain and loss. What's your testimony of life before Christ?

This week, we want to do the hard work of letting the Lord work in our hearts to reveal in our lives the things about our old life that need to be put off. This is essential work for the miracle of putting on the new life that's only possible in Jesus.

Crepe Myrtles can be beautiful trees, but they require regular maintenance. In order for them to grow in the right way and to maximize the beauty of the flowers that they produce, pruning has to be done. The old growth has to be carefully identified and cut off so that new growth can occur. It's the new growth that produces the buds and the flowers that make the tree so beautiful. This week probably won't be comfortable. It may require some pruning, but it will be fruitful if you look to the Lord and allow him to have his way and to do his work in your life by identifying and removing your old life.

14

HEARING GOD'S WORD

What did (does) your old life look like? Answer the questions below to create your testimony.

In your old life, in what ways was your thinking futile (meaningless)?

In your old life, how was your understanding darkened?

In your old life, how did you know that you were alienated from God?

In your old life, how was your heart hard towards the things of God?

In your old life, what impurities (sin) did you desire and pursue?

APPLYING GOD'S WORD

Look through the lists above, and answer this question.

What things about your old life are still a part of your life today?

RESPONDING TO GOD'S WORD

This week is about identifying sin and then confessing (admitting) and repenting (turning away) from that sin. It's a simple assignment, but it's only by God's grace and power that it can be completed. Respond to what's still in your life by confessing and repenting of your sin, trusting in Jesus Christ's death for your sin and his resurrection in victory over sin. Ask for God's forgiveness through Jesus, and ask him to help you put off what's left of your old life.

What sin do you need to confess? Confession means to agree with God that the thought, desire, or action is sinful.

What sin do you need to repent from? Repentance means to turn away from. It's the picture of making a U-turn and starting to go in another direction. Biblical repentance is always about turning away from sin and turning in faith and obedience to the Lord.

LIVING GOD'S WORD

Put off the old life . . .

Share your testimony of your old life with your New Life group. Ask them to pray for you and to hold you accountable for turning from these things in your life by the grace of God through Jesus.

PRAYING GOD'S WORD

This week, use Ephesians 4:17-22 to guide your time with the Lord in confessing and repenting of your sin. Ask the Lord to put off and take away anything in your thoughts, desires, and actions that don't honor him. Ask him to put off the old life that you've turned away from.

LESSON 5

THE NEW LIFE

And to be renewed in the spirit of your minds, and to put on the new self, created after the likeness of God in true righteousness and holiness.
Ephesians 4:23-24 (ESV)

How can we be renewed (made new) in the spirit of our minds? What does that mean and how does that work? The Apostle Paul just reminded the believers to not act like they did before they believed in Jesus. Prior to Christ, their minds – way of thinking – was meaningless and deceived. Their hearts were hard and callous to the things of the Lord. Paul reminded them to live and to grow in the new life that they received in Jesus. In other words, they needed to grow in the new heart and mind they had in Christ, so that their minds – way of thinking – would be meaningful and truthful, and they would be receptive to the things of God in their lives. How is that possible? How does that work?

Read these verses from the English Standard Version (ESV) translation of the Bible, and see if you can identify how new life – a new heart and mind – is possible:
- **Psalm 51:10** - "Create in me a clean heart, O God, and renew a right spirit within me."
- **Ezekiel 11:19** - "And I will give them one heart, and a new spirit I will put within them. I will remove the heart of stone from their flesh and give them a heart of flesh."
- **Ezekiel 36:26** - "And I will give you a new heart, and a new spirit I will put within you. And I will remove the heart of stone from your flesh and give you a heart of flesh."
- **Romans 12:2** - "Do not be conformed to this world, but be transformed by the renewal of your mind, that by testing you may discern what is the will of God, what is good and acceptable and perfect."
- **Ephesians 2:10** - "For we are his workmanship, created in Christ Jesus for good works, which God prepared beforehand, that we should walk in them."
- **Colossians 3:10** - "and have put on the new self, which is being renewed in knowledge after the image of its creator."
- **Titus 3:5** - "He saved us, not because of works done by us in righteousness, but according to his own mercy, by the washing of regeneration and renewal of the Holy Spirit."

How is the new life possible? It's only possible through God! It's the miracle of salvation, and it's the work of God through his mercy that he gives us new hearts and new minds that have been redeemed and are able to understand his truth and are able to desire to obey him! What we believe and what we think always impacts what we do. So renewing the spirit of our minds through God's Word is essential to putting on the new life in the likeness of God. Allowing the Lord to change what we believe and how we think will always impact what we do for his glory.

HEARING GOD'S WORD

What does (could) your new life look like? Answer the questions below to create your testimony.

In your new life, what does it mean to be renewed in the spirit of your minds? How is it different from your old life?

In your new life, how are you putting on the new self?

In your new life, in what ways are you growing to imitate God?

In your new life, how is true righteousness a part of your life?

In your new life, how is the Lord growing you in holiness?

APPLYING GOD'S WORD

Look through the lists above, and answer these questions.

The new life is only possible because of God's love and grace for us in Jesus. How does that make you feel towards the Lord?

What role does God's Word play in renewing your mind and putting on the new life?

RESPONDING TO GOD'S WORD

This week is about identifying how God has and is changing you, taking off the old life and putting on your new life in Christ. Just like last week, it's a simple assignment, but it's only by God's grace and power that it can be completed. Praise and thank the Lord for the changes that he's made in your thoughts, desires, and actions by giving you new life in Jesus. Ask the Lord to continue to grow you in his likeness. Commit to get into God's Word to allow his truth to renew your mind each and every day.

What change in your thinking, attitudes, or behavior do you need to thank God for this week? Take time to write down the changes he's made (making) in your life, and then give him thanks!

What change in your thoughts, desires, or actions do you want the Lord to make, to help you look more like him in your life? Ask him to make those changes in your life.

LIVING GOD'S WORD

Put on the new life . . .

This week, put your old life testimony and your new life testimony together. Go back to the person you shared your old life testimony with last week, and now share your new life testimony with them. Perhaps this week, the Lord has revealed that you don't have a new life testimony. If that's the case, ask your group leader about how you can receive the gift of new life in Jesus Christ. If you repent and turn in faith to Jesus, that's where every new life testimony begins!

PRAYING GOD'S WORD

This week, use Ephesians 4:23-24 to guide your time with the Lord in praising him and asking him for his work of making you look more like Jesus. Continue to ask the Lord to put off and take away anything in your thoughts, desires, and actions that don't honor him. Ask him to put on the new life that you now desire.

LESSON 6

NEW LIFE: SPEAK THE TRUTH

Therefore, having put away falsehood, let each one of you speak the truth with his neighbor, for we are members one of another.
Ephesians 4:25 (ESV)

What does the new life in Jesus look like? It looks like Jesus, and one of the key characteristics of Jesus is that he is the truth, the life, and the way (John 14:6). God cannot lie. This truth is stated explicitly in several places in the Bible:

- **Numbers 23:19** - "God is not man, that he should lie, or a son of man, that he should change his mind. Has he said, and will he not do it? Or has he spoken, and will he not fulfill it?"
- **Titus 1:2** - "In hope of eternal life, which God, who never lies, promised before the ages began."
- **Hebrews 6:18** - "So that by two unchangeable things, in which it is impossible for God to lie, we who have fled for refuge might have strong encouragement to hold fast to the hope set before us."

This truth is also seen in the faithfulness of God throughout the history of the world. He's completely faithful to do what he said he will do. He's done it daily since the beginning of creation. He's fulfilled so many of his promises already in the world. We can count on his faithfulness to never lie and to always speak the truth, which means we can count on his promises for today and tomorrow too.

For a Christian with new life in Jesus Christ, the goal in life is now to grow in Christ, looking more-and-more like him each day. Since one of the key characteristics of God is truth, truth should identify the life of a child of God. Believers should strive to imitate God's truth by speaking the truth to each other. Believers should strive to look like Jesus by putting away falsehood or telling lies. Why? One of the reasons is that telling lies to other believers is like lying to ourselves. Lies hurt others, ourselves, and Christ, who is in us and joins us together with other believers. We are members one of another!

So the call in Ephesians 4:25 is simple and important: Tell the truth!

This week, let's focus on letting God examine our hearts and help us put away falsehood. Let's ask the Lord to help us speak the truth to our neighbors. Let's remind ourselves of how God has connected us together as believers, joining us as members of his family in the body of Christ, which is the church.

HEARING GOD'S WORD

Using Ephesians 4:25, fill in the blanks below and discuss what God is saying to us in each of these things that's mentioned in verse 25:

- **Having put away _____,**

- **Let each one of you _____ the _____ with his neighbor,**

- **For we are _____ one of another.**

APPLYING GOD'S WORD

Look through the verse above, and answer these questions.

When are you most tempted to tell falsehoods (lies)? What was the last lie you told? Why?

Why is it sometimes hard to speak the truth to others? What are some circumstances where you have a hard time telling others the truth? Why?

What's important about remembering or considering our relationship to others when it comes to telling lies and telling the truth? What's special about the relationship that Christians have with one another?

RESPONDING TO GOD'S WORD

This week is about identifying falsehood or lies in your life and then taking steps to put off lies and put on truth in your new life in Christ. Again, remember that it's only by God's grace and power that this can be done in our lives. It's a process, but the more we put on truth and the more we take off falsehood by his strength, the more Christ grows in us, changing us to look more like him. Ask the Lord to grow you in his truth. Commit to do the hard work of putting off falsehood and speaking truth each day this week.

What lies are you living, telling others either in words or by what you're covering up and trying to hide in your life? Take time to write down the lies that the Lord reveals to you. Share these with your mentor this week, and if there are specific people you need to talk with about how you've been lying to them, do it this week.

This week, ask the Lord each day to help you speak the truth. In your conversations with others and even in your thoughts throughout each day, constantly ask God to give you a desire to be honest in all you say and do.

LIVING GOD'S WORD

Put on the new life . . .

This week, take time to really allow the Lord to identify lies in your life. Do the hard work of confessing those lies to others, and then start the wonderful journey of learning to speak the truth to others.

PRAYING GOD'S WORD

This week, use Ephesians 4:25 to guide your time in prayer with the Lord, continuing to ask him to make you look more like Jesus. Continue to ask the Lord to put off falsehood in your life, changing your thoughts, desires, and actions to reflect the Lord's truth. Ask him to put on the new life of honesty and truth in all that you desire and do. Pray that he would help you see your relationship with others through your faith and life in Jesus, and because of that, pray Ephesians 4:25 over someone else this week. Think of someone who is living a lie, and begin to pray for God's saving work in their life!

NEW LIFE: ADDRESS ANGER

Be angry and do not sin; do not let the sun go down on your anger,
and give no opportunity to the devil.
Ephesians 4:26-27 (ESV)

Anger is an emotion that we all feel. The definition of anger provided by *Oxford Languages* is "a strong feeling of annoyance, displeasure, or hostility." We've all been there. At times we know exactly what triggered anger in our hearts, and at other times, we find ourselves angry over little things that shouldn't make us angry. Sometimes, we even get angry with ourselves for being angry, but often, anger tempts us to say or do things that we know we shouldn't say or do. We've probably all said or done something that hurt someone else simply because we gave into anger and acted in sin. *This week is about identifying and addressing anger to avoid sin.*

In Ephesians 4:26, Paul said "be angry," acknowledging that this is an emotion that we all feel and can't avoid in life. Sometimes our anger is even justified, such as when we feel anger over injustice and evil in the world. We may watch the news and hear about a war, an act of terrorism, or a violent crime, and we find ourselves feeling a mix of emotions that almost always includes anger. Sometimes our anger isn't justified, such as when we're angry because someone else got something that we wanted or things didn't go just as we planned. Anger is an emotion that we all have, and so we need to learn to identify it when it creeps up in our hearts.

Paul, however, also said "be angry and do not sin." That's the key, isn't it? In the new life in Christ, we want to grow to be more like Jesus. At times, he was angry, but he never sinned. He spoke of anger in our lives as well, giving us an important warning in Matthew 5:21-24:

> "You have heard that it was said to those of old, 'You shall not murder; and whoever murders will be liable to judgment.' But I say to you that everyone who is angry with his brother will be liable to judgment; whoever insults his brother will be liable to the council; and whoever says, 'You fool!' will be liable to the hell of fire. So if you are offering your gift at the altar and there remember that your brother has something against you, leave your gift there before the altar and go. First be reconciled to your brother, and then come and offer your gift."

Jesus reminded us of the danger of anger that can lead to sin that hinders our worship of the Lord. Jesus laid the foundation for dealing with anger in a timely way: "Leave your gift there before the altar and go." Paul built on this foundation in Ephesians 4 when he said, "Do not let the sun go down on your anger, and give no opportunity to the devil." In other words, deal with anger in a timely way, not letting it simmer in your hearts and tempt you to sin. Deal with anger quickly for the purpose of reconciliation, not allowing anger to destroy love and grow hate.

Using Ephesians 4:26-27, fill in the blanks below and discuss what God is saying to us about anger in these verses:

- **Be _____ and do not _____;**

- **Do not let the _____ go down on your _____,**

- **And give no _____ to the _____.**

Look through the verses above, and answer these questions.

When are you most tempted to anger? What are some of the things that stir up anger in your heart on a regular basis? Is there anger in your heart today? What, and why?

In what ways do you often sin when you're angry (cussing, yelling at others, saying hurtful things, hurting yourself, getting drunk, etc.)?

Do you avoid dealing with anger? Do you "let the sun go down," often not dealing with anger in a timely way? Why? What's the problem with not dealing with anger?

Has the devil ever been successful in tempting you into sin when you were angry? How?

This week is about identifying and addressing anger to avoid sin. The thing that you're called to put off is sinful anger and harboring anger in your heart, which leads to sin. You're called to put on God's design for dealing with anger, which is following Christ's example and growing in your new life in Christ. Again, remember that it's only by God's grace and power that this can be done. It's a process, but the more you deal with anger in a timely way and with a focus on reconciliation, the more the Lord will continue to grow you to look more like him. Ask the Lord to grow you to be angry but not to sin. Commit to deal with anger in a timely way and with a heart for reconciliation any time anger creeps into your heart this week.

What are you angry about this week? Is there someone you feel anger towards? What do you need to do to follow Jesus' design for dealing with that anger in your life? Take time to write down the anger that the Lord reveals to you. Share these with your mentor this week, and if there are specific people you need to be reconciled with, pray for them and talk to them this week.

LIVING GOD'S WORD

Put on the new life . . .

This week, take time to let the Lord identify anger in your heart. Deal with that anger so that it doesn't lead to sin – or further sin – in your life. Each day, focus on identifying anger when it starts in your heart, and then deal with that anger before the day ends, addressing it for the purpose of reconciliation.

PRAYING GOD'S WORD

This week, use Ephesians 4:26-27 to guide your time in prayer with the Lord, continuing to ask him to make you look more like Jesus. Pray that the Lord would give you strength in Christ not to sin when you're angry. Ask the Lord to give you courage to deal with anger in a timely way and not to avoid uncomfortable or difficult conversations that are needed to bring reconciliation. Plead for the Lord's protection over Satan's temptation, and ask the Lord to help you see when anger opens a door for the devil and to give you the wisdom to close that door. Thank the Lord for his goodness in helping you identify and address anger to avoid sin in your life.

LESSON 8

NEW LIFE: WORK AND SHARE

Let the thief no longer steal, but rather let him labor, doing honest work with his own hands, so that he may have something to share with anyone in need.
Ephesians 4:28 (ESV)

Paul continues to deal with the contrast between the old self and the new self in the life of a believer, and in this verse, he calls thieves to stop stealing and to start working. So let's think about what it means to be a thief or to steal.

There's an evangelist named Ray Comfort, who often asks people these questions:
  (1) Have you ever stolen anything in your life, including something really small like a pencil, a piece of gum, a downloaded song, or a couple of hours from your job? *Most will answer honestly with "yes."*
  (2) What do you call someone who steals? *Most will say that someone who steals is called a "thief."*

Ray's point isn't to judge, it's to reveal the reality of what many people can't see, which is that we're all sinners! All of us have stolen something from someone in the past. One theft – no matter how small – makes someone a thief, guilty of breaking God's law. But why do people steal? The simple answer is because of sin. In sin, we're selfish and impatient. People steal because they want something, and they want it now. People steal because they put their desires or needs above the needs of others. People steal because of selfishness and impatience. People steal because of perceived needs that are irrational, like the addict who steals to get something to sell or trade for the next fix.

In Ephesians 4:28, the Lord commanded Christians to stop stealing and to start working. God's design for the provision of our needs in life is through work. He gives all of us skills and abilities that can be used in some type of work, and our work can and should provide for our basic needs. But God doesn't stop with work providing for our basic needs; rather, he said that believers should work so that they will have something to share with others when they are in need! In other words, the church is designed to take care of its own. It's the family of God, and the Father provides for his family and provides through his family.

This week is about identifying ways that you may be stealing. It's about dealing with that sin through repentance, or turning away from the sin of stealing. This week is about growing in the new life that you have in Jesus by seeing your work in light of God's desire for your work. He desires that you do honest work, and he desires that one of the reasons that you work is not just for yourself but also for others.

HEARING GOD'S WORD

Using Ephesians 4:28, fill in the blanks below and discuss what God said about working and sharing:

- **Let the _____ no longer _____,**

- **But rather let him _____,**

- **Doing _____ work with his own hands,**

- **So that he may have something to _____**

- **With anyone in _____.**

APPLYING GOD'S WORD

Look through the verse above, and answer these questions.

Have you ever stolen anything? Why did you do it?

When you think about working, do you think about working to provide for what you need and want? What's the difference between things we need and things we want?

God wants you to work to provide for your needs and to have extra to share with others. Have you ever thought about work in those terms? What would sharing with others look like right now in your life?

RESPONDING TO GOD'S WORD

This week is about focusing on work, examining your heart for the way that you think about work and the commitment you have to work. The Lord created us to rule over creation. He created us for work, so what does that look like in your life? Also, this week is focused on why we work, moving beyond just providing for our needs to the Lord providing us with more than we need so that we have something to share with others who are truly in need. Let the Lord reveal where your heart is in relation to sharing with others.

Have you ever stolen anything? What are the ways that we can steal from others? Why do people steal?

Do you work? What's your perspective on work? Is work a necessary evil or a gift from God? Why do people work?

How are you sharing with others? Why do you think God wants us to share?

LIVING GOD'S WORD

Put on the new life . . .

This week, deal with the sin of stealing. If you need to confess to someone that you've stolen from, do it this week. If you need to make amends for something you've stolen, take care of that this week. As you work, commit all of your work to the Lord, doing your work for the Lord. Be thankful for his provision for what you need, and be eager to share with others in need! If you don't give regularly to your church, start there! Your offerings to your church go to support the work of the Lord in making disciples of Jesus Christ, often including meeting real needs in the church.

PRAYING GOD'S WORD

This week, use Ephesians 4:28 to guide your time in prayer with the Lord, continuing to ask him to grow you in the new life you have in Jesus. Consider what the Lord's revealed to you about stealing. If you are stealing in any way right now in your life, confess that to God, which means that you admit to the sin and agree with God that stealing is sin. Ask the Lord to give you a desire to work as unto the Lord in whatever work you do. Thank him for his provision that comes in so many ways each and every day, including his provision of money for the work we do so that we'll have money for the things we need. Ask him to give you a heart that's satisfied with what he provides, and ask for a heart that's eager to share with others who are in need.

LESSON 9

NEW LIFE: HEALTHY TALK

Let no corrupting talk come out of your mouths, but only such as is good for building up, as fits the occasion, that it may give grace to those who hear.
Ephesians 4:29 (ESV)

In the New Testament, the word for "corrupting" talk means rotten, worthless, unfit to use, or bad. The idea covers a range of speech, doesn't it? From cuss words that many people find offensive, to dirty jokes that degrade the sanctity of sex within marriage, to gossip and slander that hurts and harms everyone involved, corrupting talk isn't hard to find or identify. It's the kind of talk that's common in our old lives, which were identified by sin, but it's also the kind of talk that has no place in our new lives, which are identified with God's grace in Jesus Christ.

God's command is easy to understand this week: Let no corrupting talk come out of your mouths. This is something that the Lord expects his people to do, and since he expects it, we can do it through the mind of Christ that's ours by God's grace. So how do we go about eliminating corrupting talk in our lives? First, we need to identify corrupting talk that we're guilty of using and that we're prone to use. For some, that may cuss words. For others, that may be gossip or slander. For still others, it may be all of the above. What is it for you? What identified your speech in your old life? We need to know what corrupting speech is so that we can let no corrupting talk come out of our mouths.

We also need to know what speech is good for building up, sharing God's grace with those around us. For some who grew up around believers, you may know exactly what it means to speak in a way that builds others up. Perhaps you've experienced in your life as others have spoken to you in a way that displayed the grace of God and that encouraged and built up. For others who didn't grow up around believers, you may not be very familiar with this type of speech. Perhaps even when you experience today, you're cynical of the motive of why someone is speaking to you in a kind and encouraging way. We need to know what speech that's good for building up looks like, and the best way to learn what this type of speech looks like is to look to God's Word! There's no speech that's better for building up than the very words of God, and as we learn to grow in speaking to others in a way that builds up, we need to learn how to share with others God's truth from God's Word. Specifically, we need to share the gospel!

The gospel is the greatest news we can share that builds up and that passes along the grace of God. Telling others about Jesus – his death for our sin, his burial, and his resurrection in victory over sin and death – is the good news of God's grace. There's no speech that's better for building up. So this week, when you're tempted to let corrupting talk come out of your mouth, think about and talk about Jesus!

HEARING GOD'S WORD

Using Ephesians 4:29, fill in the blanks below and discuss what God said about identifying corrupting talk and speaking to build up one another:

- **Let no _____ _____ come out of your mouths,**

- **But only such as is _____ for _____ up,**

- **As fits the _____,**

- **That it may give _____ to those who hear.**

APPLYING GOD'S WORD

Look through the verse above, and answer these questions.

What is corrupting talk? What are some examples of the way that we use corrupting talk? What tempts us to speak in ways that corrupt and hurt others?

What is talk that builds up? What are some examples of the way that you can speak to build up others? Why is this good? How does this share God's grace? When have you experienced this kind of speech from others?

RESPONDING TO GOD'S WORD

This week God's Word is targeting the important work of growing our speech to match the new life we have in Christ. Specifically, Ephesians 4:29 is meant to help us identify corrupting talk – so we can eliminate that from our conversations – and to help us identify speech that builds up, expressing and sharing the grace of God that we've received in our lives through Jesus. Take time to ask the Lord to examine your speech and to help you respond to his Word in obedience by his grace that's yours in Christ Jesus.

Identify and confess any corrupting talk that you know is in your life right now. Why are you tempted to speak in ways that corrupt and hurt others? What triggers your flesh to want to tear someone else down? Ask the Lord to remove these feelings from your heart and to show the clear way of escape that he's provided.

If there's someone you need to apologize to this week (You spoke to them or about them in a corrupting way), make the commitment to take care of that this week.

This week, how can you talk to others in a way that builds up and share the grace of God that you've received in Jesus? Share ideas with each other in your group, and pray every day, asking the Lord to give you a heart that's focused on speaking to others in a way that is good and that builds up.

LIVING GOD'S WORD

Put on the new life . . .

This week, identify corrupting talk in your life. If it happens, take time to immediately confess and repent of that sin to the Lord, and also apologize to the person that you spoke to or spoke about in a corrupting way. Also, throughout each day this week, think about how you can speak to others in a way that builds up rather than corrupts. Spend time thinking about each conversation you have, and ask the Lord to help you learn from each conversation about how you could share his grace in the way you talk to others. This week at church, if anyone speaks to you in a way that builds up, thank them for doing that, and let them know that you're working on that in your life. Ask them to pray for you!

PRAYING GOD'S WORD

This week, use Ephesians 4:29 to guide your time in prayer with the Lord. Remember that as you pray God's Word, which reveals his will for the lives of his children, you're praying a powerful prayer. Ask for what you know God wants in your life, and he will work in your life! Confess to the Lord any corrupting talk that you know is in your life and in your heart. Ask him to turn the desire of your heart away from talking in a way that corrupts and hurts. Ask him to give you the wisdom to know how to speak in a way that is good and that builds others up. Thank him for his grace in your life through Jesus, and ask him to use you – the things you say to others – to share his grace in Christ with others.

LESSON 10

NEW LIFE: PLEASING GOD

And do not grieve the Holy Spirit of God, by whom you were sealed for the day of redemption.
Ephesians 4:30 (ESV)

A young boy had done it. He had played with a ball in the house, even though his mother had told him many times not to do that, explaining how it was dangerous and might cause something to break in the house. As he bounced the ball around, it felt good. Nothing had broken, because he was quick enough to get to the ball before it hit anything that was fragile. In time, the boy became more and more confident in his ability to catch the ball, and he began to bounce it harder so that it would go farther and farther away, testing his speed and getting closer and closer to disaster. Again and again, disaster was averted, until it wasn't.

The ball finally went too far, too fast. The boy couldn't stop it from hitting the vase, and he couldn't catch the vase before it hit the ground. In an instant, the thrill of the game was over. It came crashing down, and the boy felt terrible about breaking the vase. Honestly, though, he felt more afraid about his mother finding out, so he made a bad situation worse. He came up with a lie to tell his mother so that perhaps he won't get in trouble for breaking the rules and breaking her vase. The boy tried his lie, but his mother already knew. She had been watching from a distance, listening through the wall as the boy had bounced the ball. She had heard the vase break and the panicked silence of her son. She knew, and as he told his lie, looking in her eyes, he knew that she knew.

Have you ever been there? The relationship of mother and son wasn't broken, but the fellowship was damaged. The boy's disobedience and his lies grieved the heart of his mother. More than the broken vase, the broken trust and dishonesty hurt her heart.

God sees everything. He knows everything. Considering those facts, it's amazing that he loves any of us, but he does. It's amazing that he saves any of us, but he does. And once we're his by his grace through faith in the person and work of Jesus Christ, we're his forever. Nothing can change that. Jesus said, "All that the Father gives me will come to me, and whoever comes to me I will never cast out" (John 6:37). He also said, "My sheep hear my voice, and I know them, and they follow me. I give them eternal life, and they will never perish, and no one will snatch them out of my hand. My Father, who has given them to me, is greater than all, and no one is able to snatch them out of the Father's hand. I and the Father are one" (John 10:27-30).

Once saved by God's grace, nothing and no-one can take away your salvation. You are sealed for the day of redemption, but as a son or daughter of God, your obedience and honesty before the Lord will either please or grieve the Lord. This week, we're challenged to learn not to grieve the Holy Spirit of God.

HEARING GOD'S WORD

Using Ephesians 4:30, fill in the blanks below and discuss what God said grieving the Holy Spirit and about the security of our new life that's eternal in Christ Jesus:

- **And do not _____ the _____ _____ of God,**

- **By whom you were _____ for the day of _____.**

APPLYING GOD'S WORD

Look through the verse above, and answer these questions.

What does it mean to grieve the Holy Spirit? What would make the Lord sorrowful, sad, or offended in terms of our attitudes, thoughts, and actions?

What does it mean that believers are "sealed" by the Holy Spirit for the day of redemption? What does this truth say about the possibility that Satan could snatch a believer away from the Lord or that believers could do something that would cause them to lose their salvation?

RESPONDING TO GOD'S WORD

This week God's Word brings a tremendous amount of encouragement and confidence into the heart of every believer, and it also communicates the sure hope of the gospel to those without Christ, calling them to repent and believe! Specifically, Ephesians 4:30 is intended to call believers to surrender in obedience to God, encouraged by the certainty of our eternal reward in Jesus Christ.

In thinking about the ways that we can grieve God, are you grieving the Holy Spirit in any way right now in your life? Do you have any attitudes, thoughts, or actions that you need to confess and turn away from today?

Are you sealed by the Holy Spirit for the day of redemption? Are you saved by God's grace through the gift of faith in the Son of God, Jesus Christ? If not or if you aren't sure, talk to your mentor today. The Lord wants his children to know without a shadow of a doubt that they are his and that the Holy Spirit protects and preserves to the end all who believe in Jesus.

LIVING GOD'S WORD

Put on the new life . . .

This week make a list of anything that may grieve the Holy Spirit in your life. Share that list with your mentor, and ask him/her to pray for you and to hold you accountable for turning away from these things as you pursue your new life in Jesus. Also, make a list of the things that you know the Lord desires in your life. Share this list with your group as well, and ask him to pray for you and to hold you accountable for turning towards these things in your life. Make the commitment this week to spend time with the Lord each day in prayer and in his Word. Go to church this week to worship the Lord and to fellowship with other believers. Share your faith this week, telling someone else about the grace of God through his Son, Jesus Christ.

PRAYING GOD'S WORD

This week, use Ephesians 4:30 to guide your time in prayer with the Lord. Confess and repent from anything that is grieving the Holy Spirit of God. Ask the Lord to give you eyes to see each day if there's any attitude, thought, or action that grieves him. Tell the Lord how much you don't want to grieve or upset him. Tell him how much you desire to please him. If you know that you are sealed for the day of redemption, thank the Lord for his grace and his promise of eternal salvation. Thank him that nothing and no-one can snatch you out of his hand. If you know that you aren't sealed, turn in repentance and faith to Jesus! Put your trust in his death for your sin and in his resurrection for your eternal life. Ask the Lord to save you by his grace through his Son, Jesus Christ.

LESSON 11

NEW LIFE: SINFUL ATTITUDES

Let all bitterness and wrath and anger and clamor and slander be put away from you,
along with all malice.
Ephesians 4:31 (ESV)

In Matthew 15:18-19, Jesus said, "But what comes out of the mouth proceeds from the heart, and this defiles a person. For out of the heart come evil thoughts, murder, adultery, sexual immorality, theft, false witness, slander." What a powerful truth!

The sinful things that we say and do come from the sinfulness that's in our hearts. As Jesus' half-brother James said, "You desire and do not have, so you murder. You covet and cannot obtain, so you fight and quarrel. . ." (James 4:2). Sinful attitudes are incredibly dangerous because left unchecked, they always result in sinful words and actions.

This week, the Lord calls us to examine our hearts carefully and to remove any signs of the dangerous sinful attitudes that always lead to hurtful, sinful words and actions in our lives. Like a visit to the dentist, this week may not be comfortable, but it will be helpful.

One of the keys this week is going to be taking the time to really study and to understand the differences between the various sinful attitudes and actions that are listed in Ephesians 4:31. Some of these words are closely related and have a lot of similarity, but the nuanced differences are important. Don't skip the process of carefully understanding each word so that you can prayerfully examine your heart for each underlying attitude.

Another key is to remember that the Lord doesn't put the responsibility for removing these attitudes on any process or any other person. Ephesians 4 is spoken to the church – to each believer – and the responsibility is on the individual to simply put away sinful attitudes that aren't fitting for new life in Christ. This is important, because we live in a time that justifies bitterness and anger and wrath because of past wrongs done to us or done to others connected to us. It's not up to a counselor to work out our past hurts before we can overcome sinful attitudes. It's not up to the person who may have violated and hurt us to come clean so that we can move forward. Through Christ, we have strength and victory! Through Christ, we are new creations. Through Christ, there is no condemnation. Through Christ, we are chosen, holy, and beloved.

We have all we need in Christ to live in the new life that God's so graciously given us through his Son. Don't rely on anything or anyone else. Rely on Christ! He's enough to overcome.

Using Ephesians 4:31, fill in the blanks below and discuss what God said about sinful attitudes:

- **Let all _____ and _____**

- **And _____ and _____**

- **And _____ be put _____ from you,**

- **Along with all _____.**

There are 6 different sinful attitudes and actions that the Lord identifies in this verse. Take time to look up the definition for each of these, and in your discussion, think about practical examples of how you've experienced these things in your life.

APPLYING GOD'S WORD

Look through the verse above, and answer these questions.

Out of these 6 sinful attitudes, which one was most connected to your old life? In the way that others treated you, which one of these sinful attitudes was most hurtful to you in the past? Where do these attitudes come from in our hearts and minds?

In this verse, what's the Lord's single command for the Christian who has new life in Christ? How do we put these things away from our lives?

RESPONDING TO GOD'S WORD

This week God's Word exposes some very common, sinful attitudes in the hearts of men and women. The question is, how should we respond to this verse? If you are a believer, there's only one way to respond, which is to trust and obey the Lord. Ephesians 4:31 is intended to call believers to obedience to continue to put off the old self and to put on their new life in Jesus. There's only one way that this can be done, which is through the strength of Christ that is in and with the believer. By faith through God's grace, put off any of these sinful attitudes that may linger in your life.

Do you have any bitterness in your heart? Who do you need to forgive? What do you need to release to the Lord? Uproot and kill any bitterness in your heart today.

Do you have any wrath in your heart? Ask for the Lord's forgiveness, and turn from this deadly attitude, remembering how God's wrath against your sin was paid for and forgiven through the miraculous sacrifice of Jesus for our sin!

Do you have any anger in your heart? Who do you need to forgive? What do you need to release to the Lord? Pull it out and give it to the Lord today.

Do you have any clamor or slander in your heart? Deal with these thoughts and attitudes before they form sinful words in your mouth. Release them to the Lord, trusting that he is the righteous Judge who will make all things right in the end.

Do you have any malice in your heart? Confess that to the Lord, and repent, turning to him to let his love replace sinful malice in your heart.

LIVING GOD'S WORD

Put on the new life . . .

This week, like a gardener who diligently uproots the weeds and grass in the garden, allow the Lord to uproot sinful attitudes in your life. Where they are found, confess them to the Lord and ask him to remove them from your heart. Remember that the Lord is always with you and is at work in you. It's up to you to look to him and trust in him and depend on him. Share with your mentor and your group about what the Lord uproots in your heart this week.

PRAYING GOD'S WORD

This week, use Ephesians 4:31 to guide your time in prayer with the Lord. Confess and repent from any of these sinful attitudes that may be in your life. Remember that you can put these away through the presence and the power of the Lord who is with you and will never leave you or forsake you. Like the apostle Paul said in Galatians 2:20, "I have been crucified with Christ. It is no longer I who live, but Christ who lives in me. And the life I now live in the flesh I live by faith in the Son of God, who loved me and gave himself for me." Live in Christ today to put away the sinful attitudes lingering in your heart.

NEW LIFE: GODLY ATTITUDES

Be kind to one another, tenderhearted, forgiving one another, as God in Christ forgave you.
Ephesians 4:32 (ESV)

One day two men were talking about sharing their faith. One of the men argued with his friend over the need to train and to be intentional about sharing the gospel. His argument was simple: "You don't have to encourage two guys to talk about the baseball game their favorite team just played. It's natural. If they love baseball, they'll talk about baseball. So if someone loves Jesus, they'll talk about him."

His friend thought for a moment, and then responded: "That's true, but baseball is different from the gospel. The gospel is spiritual. It's stepping into the spiritual realm and the battlefield. It's truth that has eternal significance, and the Lord uses it to convict people of sin, judgment, and righteousness. Baseball is worldly. It's not spiritual. The things of the flesh are easy. The things of the Spirit require the power of the Spirit."

Godly attitudes are the opposite of sinful attitudes, but it's important to remember that godly attitudes aren't as natural and easy as sinful attitudes. Godly attitudes are something that only the Spirit can produce and grow in the life of a believer. Godly attitudes come to life as sinful attitudes are put to death. Godly attitudes reflect the growth of Christ in the life of a believer. Godly attitudes reveal the fruit of the Spirit produced in the life of someone who is connected to the Vine: Jesus Christ.

Like the apostle Paul in Galatians 2:20, godly attitudes are the outflow of the reality of the resurrected life in Christ, so the believer can join Paul in saying that they have been crucified with Christ! It's no longer they who live but Christ who lives in them, and the lives they now live in the flesh they live by faith in the Son of God who loved them and gave his life for them.

Ephesians 4:32 reminds us that godly attitudes should reflect the love and grace of God in the gospel. Because of God's gracious kindness towards us in sending his Son to die for our sin, we should be kind to one another. Because of God's tenderhearted mercy in loving us enough to send Jesus to die for us even while we were still sinners, we should be tenderhearted towards each other. Because of God's forgiveness of our sin through the sacrifice of his Son, we should forgive one another.

For the believer who's received God's grace in Christ Jesus, there's really no excuse for not living to share the love and grace of the Lord with those around us.

HEARING GOD'S WORD

Using Ephesians 4:32, fill in the blanks below and discuss what God said about godly attitudes:

- Be _____ to one another,

- _____,

- _____ one another,

- Just as God in Christ _____ you.

APPLYING GOD'S WORD

Look through the verse above, and answer these questions.

What does kindness look like? In a practical way, how do you practice kindness in your group? Does this kindness differ from the kindness you should show to others like coworkers, church members, or neighbors? Why, or why not?

What does it mean to be tenderhearted? What tends to harden your heart in regards to the way you feel about others? Why? How can you protect your heart from becoming hardened?

What does it mean to forgive as you've been forgiven by God in Christ? How have you been forgiven by God? What does that forgiveness look like? How do you share that kind of forgiveness? Why is it inexcusable to not forgive others if God's forgiven you?

RESPONDING TO GOD'S WORD

This week, examine your life according to these godly attitudes. Ask the Lord to reveal any unkindness, hard heartedness, or unforgiveness in your life. If he does reveal that some of these things exist in your life, take time to write them down and identify who these attitudes are directed towards. Be prepared to share with your group anything that the Lord reveals to you, and take time to pray for these godly attitudes in each other's lives.

LIVING GOD'S WORD

Put on the new life . . .

Like a farmer who waters the soil into which the seed has been planted, water the seed of God's Word in your life this week by taking steps of faith and obedience in living in these godly attitudes in your new life in Jesus. Be kind to those that the Lord sends you to this week. Be tenderhearted towards those around you, believers and unbelievers alike. Be forgiving to those who have hurt you. Faith and obedience are like water on the soil that make the seeds of God's Word take root and grow!

PRAYING GOD'S WORD

Use Ephesians 4:32 to pray for godly attitudes in your life this week. Also, commit to pray for one another, asking for the Lord's power and protection in strengthening you to look more like him!

LESSON 13

NEW LIFE: KINDNESS

Be kind to one another, tenderhearted, forgiving one another, as God in Christ forgave you.
Ephesians 4:32 (ESV)

"Be nice!"

This is a phrase most of us have probably heard (more than once!). Perhaps a parent or a teacher corrected you with this phrase when you and someone else were in the middle of treating each other in a way that wasn't "nice."

We really don't have to define what "be nice" means, do we? We know when someone is being nice and when they aren't. It's connected with more than just what they say or do, but kindness is an attitude that permeates all they say and do – or don't do! Perhaps this is why the Lord connects being kind to one another with being tenderhearted with one another. Genuine kindness is driven by a tenderheart that's not exploiting or manipulating someone for selfish purposes but is driven by genuine care and concern.

Biblically, the word kindness in this verse carries the idea of goodness and virtuousness. It also points to conduct toward others that's pleasant and kind rather than hard and hurtful. It's a word that's connected to the goodness of God in 1 Peter 2:3, and a word that in this verse in Ephesians is connected to the very grace of God towards us in Christ Jesus.

Perhaps the tenderheartedness of the Lord is summarized most concisely in Romans 5:8, where "God shows his love for us in that while we were still sinners, Christ died for us." Being nice isn't just a good thing to do in the way that we treat one another. It's the gospel thing to do. Being kind and tenderhearted is one of the ways that we display the gospel in our relationships with each other.

However, kindness and tenderheartedness are not easy. They aren't the direction that the flesh naturally leads us. In this life, we are constantly faced with sin. Even for a mature believer who is growing in Christ more-and-more, sin is constantly impacting his/her life. The sin of others is a constant drip of water on our hearts, and unless there is continual reliance on the Spirit, that drip of water can dampen kindness and tenderness in the heart of the believer.

What about you? What does kindness and tenderheartedness look like in your life? Are they growing in intensity or growing damp in this sinful world? By God's grace, presence, and strength, he can protect and grow these qualities in your new life.

HEARING GOD'S WORD

Fill in the blanks below and discuss what God's Word means.

- Be _____ to one another,

- Be _____...

Use blueletterbible.org to look these words up and to study the range of their meaning and other verses where they appear in Scripture.

APPLYING GOD'S WORD

Look through the verse above, and answer these questions.

In a practical sense, how do you see kindness and tenderheartedness displayed in someone's life?

How do we see kindness and tenderheartedness in the lives of the other people in your small group?

What are some of the things that tend to dampen kindness and tenderheartedness in your life? How can you protect against the negative effects of these things in your lives?

Who do you need to show kindness to and have a tenderheart towards this week?

RESPONDING TO GOD'S WORD

Ask the Lord to reveal the reality of where your heart is in terms of kindness and tenderheartedness. Have you allowed the world to dampen and diminish these things, negatively affecting the attitude of your heart towards others? Would you ask the Lord to protect and to grow these qualities in your life?

LIVING GOD'S WORD

Put on the new life . . .

This week, if you recognize attitudes in your heart that are unkind and not tenderhearted, take the time to identify and to write down what happened to expose those attitudes. Was it something someone did and didn't do? Was it something someone said or failed to say? Was it something else?

Work on memorizing Ephesians 4:32 so that when those attitudes emerge in your heart, you can combat them with the Word of God. Everytime you feel unkind or not tenderhearted towards someone, pray Ephesians 4:32, asking the Lord to give you this in your new life in Christ. Take time to journal how the Lord answered that prayer.

PRAYING GOD'S WORD

Would you pray this prayer, thinking deeply about and asking the Lord for these things in your life. "Father, through your Son Jesus, you revealed what true kindness and tenderheartedness look like. While I was a sinner and unworthy of your mercy and love, you loved me. You sent your Son to take the punishment for my sin upon himself on the cross. You showed me unbelievable kindness when I deserved judgment. You loved me with tenderheartedness when my heart was far from loving you. How can I show unkindness and lack tenderheartedness towards others when you've shown me these things? Lord, give me your kindness and tenderheart. Grow these in me so that I can show these to those around me in order to point them to you. Help me mature in my new life in Jesus in this way this week. I ask that for your glory, through your Son. Amen."

LESSON 14

NEW LIFE: Forgiveness

Be kind to one another, tenderhearted, forgiving one another, as God in Christ forgave you.
Ephesians 4:32 (ESV)

In addition to kindness and tenderheartedness, God calls us to forgiveness. Because of the forgiveness he's given us through his Son and our Savior Jesus Christ, we are commanded to forgive one another. That's right, commanded.

In the Greek, this verse starts with an imperative or command, which calls believers to be these things: Kind, tenderhearted, and forgiving. These aren't optional. They are commanded. The Lord expects us to forgive each other. Why? Because he forgave us in Christ!

Have you ever watched dogs fight over a bone? One dog will have the bone, gnawing on it while keeping an eye on the other dog. It will even position its body in such a way to protect that bone, growling or snapping at the other dog if it gets too close. If given the chance, however, the other dog will attempt to get the bone, and if and when the other dog has the bone, it will invariably do the same thing as the first dog that had the bone, guarding and growling to protect what it has. This is the dog-eat-dog mentality. What's mine is mine, and what's yours should be mine.

This is how animals act, but it's not how humans – created as image bearers of God – should act. We do, however, apart from the new life that's only possible in Jesus. But for the believer, who has new life in Christ, we move from the way of the flesh to the way of the Spirit. Our hearts should not long to protectively guard and keep others away from what we have in Christ but to generously share and give others what we've received in Christ. One of the most significant things we've received through Jesus is forgiveness!

Forgiveness is a gift from God through his grace. It is something that becomes ours when we receive that gift, but it's not something that we can selfishly keep from others. A huge part of leading others to see the truth of God's gracious forgiveness through his Son Jesus is to share grace-driven forgiveness with one another.

So don't be like a dog with forgiveness, but be like our Lord, who sent his Son to die for us even while we were sinners so that he might extend true and complete forgiveness to us – a forgiveness that we could never deserve.

HEARING GOD'S WORD

Fill in the blanks below and discuss what God's Word means.

- _____ one another,

- As God in Christ _____ you.

How did God in Christ forgive you?

How do you extend to others the forgiveness that God gave you?

APPLYING GOD'S WORD

Look through the verse above, and answer these questions.

Have you been forgiven by God in Christ? How? How do you know that's true in your life?

Is there anyone that you need to forgive? Who, and why? Share with your group, and pray for one another. How do you need to communicate your forgiveness to that person?

RESPONDING TO GOD'S WORD

If you are holding unforgiveness in your heart, that's sin. There's no other way to see it as God clearly commanded us to forgive. So if that's you, confess your sin and repent of your sin by walking in obedience to the Lord. By faith, forgive! If you are able, extend that forgiveness to the person you've been holding unforgiveness against. Additionally, if you've been forgiven by God in Christ, take time to think about how deep and undeserved that forgiveness truly is! Think about the worst things you've thought, said, and done. Consider the things you've failed to say and do that you know the Lord desired in your life. Praise and worship the Lord for his rich mercy in forgiving us in such an unmerited way through his Son Jesus.

LIVING GOD'S WORD

Put on the new life . . .

This week, write down the names of anyone you need to forgive. Now go and extend forgiveness to these people.

How did that go? Were you able to share your forgiveness with them? How did they receive the news that you forgave them?

Why is this important to do even if you're not able to share forgiveness with the person (dead or lost contact with them), or they don't receive your forgiveness well?

PRAYING GOD'S WORD

Meditate on Ephesians 4:32, considering the fact of God's forgiveness through Christ. Praise and worship the Lord for his forgiveness that's such a display of his undeserved kindness and tenderheartedness towards us. Ask God to protect your heart against unforgiveness. Whenever you feel an attitude of unforgiveness creeping up in your life, quote Ephesians 4:32 and recount the forgiveness of the Lord in your life. Ask God to grow your new life in Christ by giving you a heart of forgiveness in order to share and to point others to the true forgiveness that's only found in Jesus.

LESSON 15

NEW LIFE: Love

Therefore be imitators of God, as beloved children. 2 And walk in love, as Christ loved us and gave himself up for us, a fragrant offering and sacrifice to God.
Ephesians 5:1-2 (ESV)

Children imitating a parent can be either something that's endearing or something that's embarrassing. It all depends on what they are imitating! But in most cases, it's fun and wonderful for most of us to see children who imitate their parents. But why do they imitate their parents?

This is what they see and learn, for sure, but for many children, it's also who they love and admire. In the best case, a child loves and admires their parent(s). They look up to them, and when they are young, their parents become someone they want to be like. When mom or dad react a certain way when they are excited, so does the child. When mom and dad react a certain way when they are sad, so does the child. This imitation is a part of learning and growing.

So when we come to Ephesians 5:1, this basic experience in life – which exists in every culture in every age – becomes the illustration for our reaction to our heavenly Father. If we are beloved children, then we should imitate our Father! Kindness, tenderheartedness, and forgiveness all are done in imitation of God, and so is the way we love.

The Lord connects love to the gospel in Ephesians 5:2. This is the way that God proved his love to us, and it's the expression of true, sacrificial, and life-giving love. Christ loved us enough that he willingly gave himself as a sacrifice for our sin. It was a fragrant offering that pleased and satisfied God. It was a sacrifice, given because of our sin and for our sin. Love is seen in the fact that Jesus gave his life for sin. No one took his life. The Jews didn't conquer him. He sacrificed his life, willingly going to the cross to bear the weight of God's judgment against our sin. What a picture of love!

Love isn't just a feeling of excitement and interest between people. It's not just chemical reactions in our bodies that produce something we experience. Love is a decision. Love is a commitment. Love is sacrificial and giving. Love is obedience. Love is found in the person and work of Jesus.

In our new life in Christ, we are called to imitate God, and one of the key characteristics that we are commanded to imitate is love.

HEARING GOD'S WORD

Fill in the blanks below and discuss what God's Word means.

- **Therefore be _____ of God,**

- **As _____ _____.**

- **And walk in _____,**

- **As Christ _____ us and _____ himself up for us,**

- **A fragrant _____ and _____ to God.**

APPLYING GOD'S WORD

Look through the verse above, and answer these questions.

Considering verse 1, are you a beloved child of God through your relationship to the Son of God Jesus?

What does it look like to imitate God? In a very practical way, discuss what you did and said yesterday. In what ways did you imitate God? In what ways did you not imitate God?

According to verse 2, how is the love of Christ defined? What are some characteristics of this love that are important to know?

What does the Lord mean when he calls us to "walk in love?"

RESPONDING TO GOD'S WORD

Memorize two words in Ephesians 5:1-2: Imitate and walk. Both of these words denote action. To imitate means to follow the pattern and example of someone else, mimicking what they say and do. To walk means to actually live out something, walking or doing the thing that you are called to walk out or live out. Everyday, meditate on these two things in your life, asking yourself throughout each day, "Am I imitating God by walking in love in this situation, in my speech, and in my actions?"

LIVING GOD'S WORD

Put on the new life . . .

As you meditate on imitating God and walking in his love, keep a journal this week to record the things that the Lord teaches you about imitating him and walking in his love.

What are some ways that you were challenged to imitate God and walk in his love?

What are some ways that you were blessed by imitating God and walking in his love?

PRAYING GOD'S WORD

Using Ephesians 5:1-2, pray for the following things:
- *That your identity through Christ as a beloved child of God would be the truth that drives the way you see yourself;*
- *That by the power of the Holy Spirit, you would imitate God more-and-more in your life;*
- *That by God's grace, you would be able to walk in love of Christ everyday; and*
- *That for God's glory, he would use your life and witness to share the love of Christ with those around you.*

LESSON 16

NEW LIFE: Purity

*But sexual immorality and all impurity or covetousness must not even be
named among you, as is proper among saints.*
Ephesians 5:3 (ESV)

Turn on the TV to any major network for primetime programming in the evening, and without a doubt, you will be exposed to a host of things that are sexually immoral, that are impure, and that prompt and encourage covetousness.

Everyday, TV programming fills homes and hearts with the message that the only thing that's sexually immoral is non-consensual, exploitative, and abusive sexual activity. Otherwise, the message that's aggressively campaigned is that everything goes when it comes to sex. There's hardly a show on today that doesn't normalize gay and lesbian marriage, gender identity, and sexual promiscuity.

Added to this on-slaught of sexual immorality is every impurity. Nothing is sacred, especially the view of God and the truth of God. On these same shows, Christianity is often displayed as backwards and hateful. Christians are shown as the ones who are often cast as being responsible for hate crimes and for exploitative and abusive acts. Christians are very often cast as the ones driven by bigotry against sexual sin and race. The Scriptures are twisted, and the reality of true Christianity is hidden. The result is the greatest impurity there is: Dishonoring and distorting the truth of God and his Word.

Finally, in all of these ways, TV mirrors the sin in the world around us. It magnifies sin in an exceptional way, by glorifying the world and the things of the world in such a way that leads hearts to covet what they see on TV in the make-believe lives of characters in these shows. TV shows often draw hearts to desire the things of the flesh, promoting the false idea that only the things of this world are real and matter and that pursuing those things will be what brings real happiness and completion.

God made it clear in Ephesians 5:1-2 where Christians should stand in relationship to these things: They shouldn't even be named among us! In other words, these things shouldn't be a topic of conversation. The details of these sins shouldn't be what we like to discuss and talk about. Our minds and hearts shouldn't be occupied with these things and finding some satisfaction in thinking and talking about these things.

Why? Because we are saints! We have been set aside and made holy unto the Lord. In Christ, we have been made righteous and identified as God's holy ones! We are his saints.

HEARING GOD'S WORD

Fill in the blanks below and discuss what God's Word means.

- But _____ immorality and

- All _____

- Or _____

- Must not even be _____ among you,

- As is proper among _____.

APPLYING GOD'S WORD

Look through the verse above, and answer these questions.

Biblically, what is sexual immorality?

How is sexual immorality different from all impurity?

Define covetousness. How does the world around us prompt covetousness?

What does it mean to not name something? What's the point that God wants us to get?

Look up the definition of saint. The New Testament applies this term to every believer.

RESPONDING TO GOD'S WORD

Respond to the following questions, and prepare to share your responses with your group:
- *Are you practicing any form of sexual immorality? If so, what? How have you struggled with this in your life?*
- *Are you watching, listening to, reading, or allowing any other impurities to be a regular part of your life? If so, what? How can one walk in obedience by walking away from these things?*
- *Do you struggle with covetousness in any way? If so, how, and what? What would it take to find your satisfaction and contentment in Christ?*
- *Do you have a hard time seeing yourself as God's saint? Why, or why not?*

LIVING GOD'S WORD

Put on the new life . . .

This week, as you encounter temptation or struggle with sexual immorality, impurity, or covetousness, reach out to someone in your group to ask for their prayer and to talk with them about God's truth in these verses. We all need accountability and encouragement in our faith. Also, if you do encounter temptation and struggle, read and reread Ephesians 5:3, reminding yourself that you are a saint through Christ! These things are completely opposite and opposed to who you are and all you have in Christ. Why settle for a cheap imitation when you have the real thing!

PRAYING GOD'S WORD

Use Ephesians 5:3 to pray for others in your group and for your family and your church. Focus on the children and youth in your family and church. They live in an age where they are constantly bombarded with sexual immorality, impurity, and covetousness. Pray for the Lord's protection and victory in their minds and hearts, and ask for opportunities to talk with those you know about what the Lord said in Ephesians 5:3.

LESSON 17

NEW LIFE: Purity in Speech

Let there be no filthiness nor foolish talk nor crude joking, which are out of place,
but instead let there be thanksgiving.
Ephesians 5:4 (ESV)

It rang out across the playground. Words that all could hear shouted in anger and defiance: "Sticks and stones may break my bones, but words will never hurt me." There's probably no phrase that young children say that's more deceptive than these.

The fact is, words have tremendous power and cause a tremendous amount of hurt and pain. There's probably not a single one of us who can't think of something somebody said at sometime in our lives that still brings hurt or anger or both into our heart when we think about those words. Words matter because words express the heart of the speaker. Hurtful words aren't always words that are directly hurtful and painful. Hurtful words are often words that were spoken in deception and words that were manipulated and exploited. Hurtful words are often words that are foolish and crude, making fun of others for selfish enjoyment and without regard to the damage and pain that they cause.

For the Lord's saints, our words matter.

In Ephesians 5:4, the Lord reminds of this truth and calls his children to imitate him in the way they speak by not using filthy, foolish, and crude speech. These things are "out of place." In other words, they don't belong in the life of a believer. They are as out of place as a fish on a football field, a knitting nettle on a sewing machine, and a pile of ketchup on a filet mignon. They don't belong in the mouths and conversations of God's children.

So what does belong in the mouths of saints? According to Ephesians 5:4, the answer to that question is "thanksgiving!"

The gospel and our new life in Christ transforms our speech, filling it with thanksgiving. You are a saint only by God's grace and the work of Jesus in his death and resurrection. You are a beloved child of God only by God's grace through the gift of faith in Jesus. You are forgiven only by the atoning work of Christ, who died for your sin, and through the tender mercy of the Lord who loved you enough to send his Son to die for your sin.

We could go on-and-on, but the point is simple. We've been given new life in Jesus, so why in the world would we want to return to or hold on to aspects of our old life? We should think often of all we've received in Christ in order to give God thanks often for our new life in Jesus.

HEARING GOD'S WORD

Fill in the blanks below and discuss what God's Word means.

- **Let there be no** _____

- **Nor** _____ **talk**

- **Nor** _____ **joking,**

- **Which are** _____ **of** _____ **,**

- **But instead let there be** _____ **.**

APPLYING GOD'S WORD

Look through the verse above, and answer these questions.

In general, what are examples or topics of filthy speech? What makes that speech filthy?

Define the word foolish. What are examples of foolish talk?

What does crude joking refer to?

What is thanksgiving? Why is it important – and appropriate – that a believer's speech be filled with thanksgiving? How does thankful speech help guard against these other types of inappropriate speech?

RESPONDING TO GOD'S WORD

Some people talk a lot, and some people talk a little. For both groups – and everyone in-between – there's one thing that's true: Our speech matters to our Lord. This week, think about what you say. Think about what you say before you say it, and reflect on what you've said. In all your speech, ask the Lord to protect you from filthy, foolish, and crude talk. In all your speech, try to thank the Lord in some way in every conversation. That's not hard to do, because the Lord is responsible for every good thing in everyone's life, and he's the hope for every need in every life. So this week, respond by filling your speech with thanksgiving.

LIVING GOD'S WORD

Put on the new life . . .

As you go through the week to come, pay careful attention to your speech. Keep a journal to record times that you were tempted or failed in protecting your speech from filthy, foolish, and crude talk. Why were you tempted, or why did you give in? What was the source of your temptation (desire to fit in with others, a fear of the rejection of others, etc.)?

To help you focus on the speech the Lord deserves and desires, ask the Lord to fill your speech with thanksgiving, and to help with this, make a list everyday of the ways that you can give thanks to the Lord. Include in your journal the opportunities and ways that you were able to give thanks to the Lord in the conversations that you had throughout the week. This is the pattern of speech for your new life in Jesus!

PRAYING GOD'S WORD

Use Ephesians 5:4 to pray for the speech of those in your group as well as for yourself. Ask the Lord to change your hearts to be repulsed by filthy, foolish, and crude speech. Ask the Lord to open your eyes to see all the things that you have to be thankful for each and every day. For the Lord's glory through your new life, ask God to help you grow to give him thanks in every conversation, helping to keep your words pure for your witness for him.

NEW LIFE: Protection from Deception

For you may be sure of this, that everyone who is sexually immoral or impure, or who is covetous (that is, an idolater), has no inheritance in the kingdom of Christ and God. 6 Let no one deceive you with empty words, for because of these things the wrath of God comes upon the sons of disobedience. 7 Therefore do not become partners with them; 8 for at one time you were darkness, but now you are light in the Lord. Walk as children of light….
Ephesians 5:5-8 (ESV)

There were gasps across the room as the man sawed the box in half because just a few seconds before a woman had gotten into the box. Her head was sticking out of one end, and her feet were dancing and moving outside of the other end of the box. Before long, the man was finished sawing and spread the two boxes apart! The lady was still smiling and her feet were still dancing, although they were completely disconnected in two separate boxes that were now several feet apart from one another on the stage. The gasps turned to cheers as the man put the two boxes together again, opened the lid, and the women emerged unhurt.

Children love magic tricks. There's a wonder and excitement in seeing something happen that is naturally and normally impossible. But all magic tricks have one thing in common, and that one thing is deception. The magic isn't real; it's a trick. There's a deception that produces the trick. "Smoke and mirrors and misdirection" are the common ways to describe how the deception occurs, and the purpose of deception is simple. Make people believe that they see one thing when in actuality, another thing that they can't see is what is really happening.

God doesn't want his children to be deceived, and the new life he gives us in Christ is intended to grow us to see through the deception in this world. In Ephesians 5:6, the Lord said "Let no one deceive you…!"

What is the deception that he's talking about? He's talking about the deception that the wrath of God isn't coming against sin. This is the lie of the world. They say, "Look at me. I have sex with who I want, and I say what I want, and I have all these things that you don't have. Where's the Lord's wrath?"

These verses remind us that those who live in persistent sin will not inherit the kingdom of God. In fact, the wrath of God is coming on account of these things. The world's deception is empty words, and those words have no real meaning and significance. It's smoke and mirrors and misdirection that's intended to pull hearts away from what's really true.

So how are we to respond? God's direction is simple: Don't partner with them by walking in the darkness. Walk in the light of Christ because through Jesus you are children of light!

HEARING GOD'S WORD

Fill in the blanks below and discuss what God's Word means.

- **For you may be sure of this, that everyone who is _____ immoral**

- **Or _____,**

- **Or who is _____ (that is, an idolater),**

- **Has _____ inheritance in the _____ of Christ and God.**

- **Let no one _____ you with empty words,**

- **For because of _____ things the _____ of God comes upon the sons of disobedience.**

- **Therefore do not become _____ with them;**

- **For at one time you were _____,**

- **But now you are _____ in the Lord.**

- **Walk as children of _____.**

APPLYING GOD'S WORD

Look through the verse above, and answer these questions.

What's the deception that the Lord warns us about in these verses? How do you see the evidence of that deception in the world?

When it talks of God's wrath that comes against the sons of disobedience, what does that mean? Who are sons of disobedience? What is the wrath of God?

What does it mean that you (a believer) once walked in darkness? When was that in your life?

What does it mean to walk in the light? What is a child of the light?

RESPONDING TO GOD'S WORD

Are you partnered in any way with those who walk in darkness? If so, in what way? How do you need to deal with that partnership in your life? Are you a child of light? If so, how? How is walking in the light connected to your new life in Jesus? This week, deal with partnerships with the world that are against God's design for your life as his saint and his child, and focus on walking in the light in Christ.

LIVING GOD'S WORD

Put on the new life . . .

Make a list of the partnerships with the world that are unhealthy in your life. How can you deal with this biblically and in faith? Keep a journal of what steps you took to deal with these partnerships. How did you share your faith and point others to the gospel through taking these steps of obedience?

Take one day to record everything that you said and did that was reflective of walking in the light. How did a focus on walking in the light of Christ and living as a child of light impact your thoughts, words, and actions that day? This is a part of your new life in Jesus.

PRAYING GOD'S WORD

Thank the Lord for his goodness and mercy in warning us about this dangerous deception in the world. Pray for the protection of the hearts of others in your group and in your church. Ask the Lord to shine the light of his truth fully and brightly in your life so that you can see and walk in the light of Christ in every way. Thank him for making you a child of light by his mercy and grace in Christ Jesus.

LESSON 19

NEW LIFE: Hope in Inheritance

For you may be sure of this, that everyone who is sexually immoral or impure, or who is covetous (that is, an idolater), has no inheritance in the kingdom of Christ and God. 6 Let no one deceive you with empty words, for because of these things the wrath of God comes upon the sons of disobedience. 7 Therefore do not become partners with them; 8 for at one time you were darkness, but now you are light in the Lord. Walk as children of light….
Ephesians 5:5-8 (ESV)

In an old family cemetery, there stands a tombstone over a grave that lists the name of the children who paid for the tombstone in memory and honor of their father. At the end of the list, it says "except for…," and then lists the name of one final sibling. That sibling was written off the list, perhaps because they failed to contribute to the cost of the tombstone. They didn't have a share in the credit for the monument that honored their father. Perhaps, they didn't have an inheritance because their choices in life had separated them from their father and their family.

Inheritances are meaningful and important to most people. Sometimes, the inheritance is sizable and significant in terms of monetary value. Most of the time – regardless of the financial value – an inheritance is special because it represents a part of the person that you were connected to, serving as a reminder that the person loved you and wanted to leave you something special when they left this earth.

Ephesians 5:5-8 talks of an inheritance, but it's not focused on an inheritance that's received. Rather, it's focused on an inheritance that's not received. The point of this warning is that those who practice sexual sin, impurity, and covetousness will not have an inheritance in the kingdom of God. These words from our Lord are in direct contradiction to the world's words that say you can live in sexual sin and go to heaven. God's Word says the opposite, and it warns believers not to be deceived.

Persistent, unrepentant sin is often the clearest evidence of an unrepentant, unregenerate heart. On the other hand, repentance and the desire for obedience is often the clearest evidence of a repentant, regenerate heart. The Lord hasn't made it complicated. His words in these verses remind us of that fact, and they warn us of the common deception to which some fall prey. Don't be deceived! But for those who are children of light, there is an inheritance in the kingdom of Christ and God.

This is our hope in this life! This is the truth that grows hope in our hearts. This life is not the end, nor is it the reality that matters most. There's life after life on earth, which is eternal life and not life counted by years. Walk as children of light who walk in the light because we know the light of the world: Jesus Christ!

Fill in the blanks below and discuss what God's Word means.

- **For you may be sure of this, that everyone who is sexually immoral or impure, or who is covetous (that is, an idolater), has _____ _____ in the _____ of Christ and God.**

- **For at one time you were _____, but now you are _____ in the Lord.**

APPLYING GOD'S WORD

Look through the verse above, and answer these questions.

What does your walk reveal: Are you a child of disobedience or are you a child of light?

Think about those who are living in idolatry. What does God say about the reality of their eternal state? Do you truly believe this? What does that truth make you want to do?

Do you remember when you were in the darkness? What kind of hope did you have at that time? What were the things that you were putting your hope in?

As a child of light, you have an eternal inheritance. How does this bring hope into your life? How often do you think about your eternal inheritance? How often do you share your eternal inheritance? It's the only inheritance there is that doesn't diminish no matter how many siblings you have!

RESPONDING TO GOD'S WORD

Take time to pray for those who have no inheritance in the kingdom of Christ and God. Ask for the Lord's mercy and salvation in their lives. Ask him for the courage and effectiveness to share your hope in Christ with them. Think about and thank God for the hope of your inheritance in the kingdom of Christ and God. There's no greater hope. There's no richer reward. There's nothing that compares in life or death. Christ is our only hope!

LIVING GOD'S WORD

Put on the new life . . .

Everyday this week, pray for the hopeless and remember your hope. As God puts individuals on your heart or in your path, share the hope of Christ with them. Keep a list of those that you are praying for and have spoken with during the week.

PRAYING GOD'S WORD

Use Ephesians 5:5-8 has a guide for your prayer time this week for the lost and for your walk in the light of Christ. Specifically, pray that the Lord would grow and strengthen your hope in your inheritance in the kingdom of Christ and God.

LESSON 20

NEW LIFE: Exposing Sin

Take no part in the unfruitful works of darkness, but instead expose them. 12 For it is shameful even to speak of the things that they do in secret. 13 But when anything is exposed by the light, it becomes visible, 14 for anything that becomes visible is light. Therefore it says, "Awake, O sleeper, and arise from the dead, and Christ will shine on you."
Ephesians 5:11-14 (ESV)

A young boy had the opportunity to make his first trip to a hunting camp. He was with one of his friends and his friend's father, and the trip to the camp was almost as exciting as the experiences in the woods that would come during the trip. As they went further and further away from paved roads and deeper and deeper into the fields and woods that made up the landscape for the entrance to the camp, the last of daylight disappeared into darkness. The headlights on the truck were just enough to brighten the path in front of them, but as they made their way to the last big turn before the camp, the father of the young man's friend said, "Now keep your eyes open, there should be some deer up here." The young man looked intently, but all he saw was darkness on either side of the truck. At the curve, however, the father of his friend slowed the truck down and turned on his bright lights that illuminated the field in front of them. All they could see were glowing eyes looking back. To his amazement, there were dozens of deer in the field in front of the young man! Seconds earlier, without enough light, there was only darkness.

Most people love a good flashlight, but they don't love a flashlight that doesn't work well or reliably. When you need a light in the dark, you need a light that works. You need a light that's bright enough to overcome the darkness and to reveal what you can't otherwise see.

God's Word reminds us that as children of light, there's no place in our lives for participating in the unfruitful works of darkness. These works aren't defined other than by the reality that they are shameful to speak of and that they are the kinds of things that are done in secret. That description provides a clear enough guide to fill our minds with the possibilities that we know are connected to unfruitful works of darkness. From illegal to immoral activities that the world hides while they pursue, we know what the Apostle Paul had in mind.

As children of light, we shouldn't walk in the darkness. In fact, we should do the complete opposite. We should be like the bright flashlight in the darkness that exposes and reveals the unfruitfulness of sin in this world. We should be like the truck headlights on bright, shining through the darkness in a way that leaves sin glowing and exposed.

This week is about exposing sin. We should walk in the light in such a way that we continue to expose sin for the gracious purpose of God's salvation and sanctification.

HEARING GOD'S WORD

Fill in the blanks below and discuss what God's Word means.

- Take _____ part in the _____ works of _____,

- But instead _____ them.

- For it is shameful even to _____ of the things that they do in _____.

- But when anything is _____ by the _____, it becomes visible

APPLYING GOD'S WORD

Look through the verse above, and answer these questions.

As you think about unfruitful works of darkness, what are some specific examples that you find in your community?

In considering the list you came up with, do you still struggle with occasionally or frequently walking in any of these things? If so, confidentially confess this to your group. Spend time talking about how you can help one another and be accountable to one another.

How are we supposed to expose the works of darkness? What does that look like in a practical way if we're dealing with sin in the life of another believer? What about dealing with sin in the life of an unbeliever? How does the church expose the works of darkness?

RESPONDING TO GOD'S WORD

This week is a week to ask the Lord to shine the light of his truth into every nook and cranny of your life. Ask him to leave no stone unturned in searching out your heart and shining light into any area of darkness left in you. Pray with one another for this in your lives, and hold one another accountable to this in your lives. There's no place for walking in darkness for the believer. There should only be room for the light of Christ!

LIVING GOD'S WORD

Put on the new life . . .

If any areas of darkness were exposed this week in your life, write them down and confess them to someone in your small group. Shining the light and exposing the truth is the first step. There's no hiding what's been exposed!

Perhaps the Lord has put it on your heart to expose the darkness that someone else is hiding in. Who is that other person? How can you share with them in a way that's full of truth and love for the purpose of exposing the darkness that's blinded them through the light of Christ?

PRAYING GOD'S WORD

Use these verses to pray for each other this week, asking the Lord to give us power by his grace to walk in the light and to be the light in this world that exposes the darkness.

NEW LIFE: Exposing Sin

Take no part in the unfruitful works of darkness, but instead expose them. 12 For it is shameful even to speak of the things that they do in secret. 13 But when anything is exposed by the light, it becomes visible, 14 for anything that becomes visible is light. Therefore it says, "Awake, O sleeper, and arise from the dead, and Christ will shine on you."
Ephesians 5:11-14 (ESV)

In a coffin that's completely sealed so that there's not the slightest sliver of light that can get inside, it's completely dark. The dead body that lies inside the coffin can't see. It can't talk. It can't think. It's only the shell or the earthly tent of the soul that once lived in it. If there were a camera inside the coffin, we still couldn't see any of the details of the body that lay inside. It would be black grain on the screen, unable to see the changes that occur over time as the body deteriorates in darkness. This is the reality of darkness. Things in the dark aren't visible. They can't be seen without light.

Light, however, makes things visible. Even the smallest sliver of light, cuts into the darkness and allows a healthy eye to begin to see a little bit of what's there. This is beautifully seen every morning in creation as the sun rises. and the things that were just dark forms that could barely be made out through the dim light of night now become distinct, filled with color, and clearly seen. Light makes things visible, and according to John 1, Jesus Christ is the light of the world.

God reminds us in Ephesians 5 that things that become visible are light. We're able to see them only because of the light, and the Lord connects that light to Christ! The call is the call of new life in Jesus. It's the call of regeneration that leads to new life: "Awake, O sleeper, and arise from the dead, and Christ will shine on you." What words of grace and wonder! Like Jesus calling outside of the tomb of Lazarus, the Lord calls to the soul that's dead in its trespasses and sins. Awake . . . arise! What was dead in darkness now steps into the light that is Christ. The Lord's light shines into the new life of a believer, illuminating everything, allowing them to see the realities of what's there that before they simply couldn't see.

This week is a call to new life for anyone who doesn't have new life in Christ. If that's you, it's a call to awake and arise for the first time by repenting of your sin and putting your faith in Jesus Christ, who is your Savior and Lord. If you already have new life in Christ, it's a call to continue to allow Jesus – the light of the world – to shine into your life.

This week is a week to identify and to praise the Lord for the things he's opened your eyes to see and to transform in your heart. It's a week to continue to ask the Lord to shine his light into your soul, continuing to show you things he's transforming right now.

HEARING GOD'S WORD

Fill in the blanks below and discuss what God's Word means.

- **For anything that becomes _____ is _____.**

- **Therefore it says, "_____, O sleeper,**

- **And _____ from the _____,**

- **And _____ will _____ on you."**

APPLYING GOD'S WORD

Look through the verse above, and answer these questions.

When did the Lord call you to awake and arise, giving you new life in Christ? Work on sharing your testimonies with each other to help you prepare to go and share with those who need Christ.

What were some of the first things that God revealed in your life when you were saved? What were the first things that you saw that needed to be changed by his grace and power in your life? How did he make those transformations in your new life?

Is there anything right now in your life that the light of Christ is shining on and revealing to you the need for repentance and transformation? If so, what?

RESPONDING TO GOD'S WORD

This week, pray these verses daily, focusing on three things:

(1) Thanking God for calling you from darkness and into the light. Praising him for bringing you from death to life in Jesus.

(2) Asking God to open your eyes to those around you who are dead and in the darkness, and pleading with God to call them to awake and arise and to give you the courage to share your testimony with them.

(3) Opening your life to the light of Christ to continue to shine on and reveal anything that's in your life that you need to see and to submit to God.

LIVING GOD'S WORD

Put on the new life . . .

As you think about your salvation and how God's grace has changed your life, make a list of some of those specific changes. Share this list with your group this week, and if you have children or grandchildren, share it with them as well.

As the Lord puts specific people on your heart to pray for and to share the gospel with, write down their names. Share this list with your group this week, and pray for these people's salvation.

As the Lord identifies specific things that need to be transformed in your life, write down the things he's revealed. Begin to ask him to replace these things with the fruit of his Spirit. Share this list with your group and ask them to pray for the Lord's work in growing your new life in Christ.

PRAYING GOD'S WORD

Lord, thank you for calling me to awake and arise! Thank you for the light of Christ in my life that helps me see the reality of sin and that gives me power in the Spirit to walk in obedience. May my life be light that shines the light of Jesus!

NEW LIFE: Walking Wisely

Look carefully then how you walk, not as unwise but as wise, 16 making the best use of the time, because the days are evil.
Ephesians 5:15-16 (ESV)

Wisdom is knowledge that's rightly applied. It's not only knowing what to do, but it's knowing when to do it and how to do it. Wisdom is a quality that comes from God, whose every word and action is wise. In our lives, true godly wisdom comes from the Spirit. It's displayed in a life that's imitating God, and it's not just about great knowledge but about actions and words that are wise.

Wisdom grows in our lives as we grow to look carefully at how we walk. This is the first command in this verse: Look carefully! God's call is simple in this verse. Pay attention to how you are living your life and what you are saying and doing everyday. Measuring wisdom in our lives as believers isn't some deep mystery. Measuring wisdom is easy. *Am I living by God's design for my life, according to his Word?*

Having wisdom doesn't involve great knowledge in philosophy and sociology and history. Having wisdom requires God's Word. This is critical to understand because the wisdom of the world is often the opposite of the wisdom of God. The world says trust what you see. God tells us to walk by faith and not by sight (2 Corinthians 5:7). The world says to hate your enemy. God says to love your enemy and pray for those who persecute you (Matthew 5:44). The world says to get your revenge. God says to never avenge yourself but to leave it to the Lord (Romans 12:19). We could go on-and-on, but the point should be clear. God's ways aren't the world's ways (Isaiah 55:8-9)!

We live in evil days that are full of evil. None of us need to be convinced of that fact. We're reminded of evil everyday as we walk out of doors and into the schools we attend, the businesses where we work, and the community in which we live. We see how widespread evil is in this world as we scroll through news feeds on our phones or turn on the TV to catch news. As believers, these realities shouldn't shake our faith. They should actually strengthen our faith. This is exactly what God said would happen (Matthew 24:3-13; 2 Timothy 3:13; etc.)!

As believers, how do we respond? We make the most of the time we're given. Everyday is a gift from the Lord, and everyday in this evil world is an opportunity to be a light for the Lord. Everyday, we can live by God's wisdom so that our words and actions will stand out from the world's wisdom, shouting out through our walk the glory and the grace of our Creator. So look carefully at how you walk, and make the most of everyday.

Fill in the blanks below and discuss what God's Word means.

- **Look _____ then how you _____,**

- **Not as _____ but as _____,**

- **Making the _____ _____ of the time,**

- **Because the days are _____.**

These verses are worth memorizing! They are short and practical, and they provide an important reminder and direction for each and every day. Take time to discuss them, and try to memorize them so that you can meditate on God's direction for your living wisely and making the most of everyday.

APPLYING GOD'S WORD

Look through the verse above, and answer these questions.

What does it mean to look carefully at the way you walk? What are some practical ways that you can examine or study your life each day? What are things that tend to distract you or discourage you from carefully examining the things you say and do?

When you are considering what's wise and unwise, how do you determine what's wise? Do you often fail to think about whether what you're saying or doing is wise or unwise? Why? How does having close, discipling relationships with other believers help protect us from unwise directions in life?

What does it mean to make the best use of the time? Are you doing that in your life?

In making the best use of time, why are the small things just as important – if not more important – than the big things that we get the chance to accomplish or to do each day?

RESPONDING TO GOD'S WORD

This week, look carefully at your walk. Continue to ask the Lord to reveal areas of your heart and mind that need the transforming grace of Christ. Take time to write down those areas where your walk isn't wise, and ask the Lord to grow your wisdom through obedience in that area in your life. Second, ask yourself throughout every day – in every encounter you have – whether or not you are making the best use of the time. This doesn't mean that every minute must be occupied by some grand and noble act. There's a time for everything, including rest and solitude. The question of the best use of your time is a question of surrender and obedience to God's will.

LIVING GOD'S WORD

Put on the new life . . .

Look carefully at your walk. Consider keeping a journal this week to record the ups and downs of your week and to reflect on your walk. Did you walk in wisdom, imitating the Lord and following his design for your life? Record your week so that you can share, encourage, and pray for one another next week.

Make the best use of the time. As you remind yourself of these words from the Lord throughout the coming week, keep track of how the Lord uses these words to direct your walk. Take time to praise and worship him throughout the week as he helps you make the best use of the time in a way that glorifies him and points others to him.

PRAYING GOD'S WORD

Lord, the days are evil. Help me make the best use of the time that you give me here on this earth. Give me wisdom to apply your Word to my life each and every day. May my words and my actions be a reflection of you, displaying your wisdom to those around me. Give me spiritual eyes to see the reality of my walk, and conform my life more-and-more to Jesus this week.

LESSON 23

NEW LIFE: God's Will

Therefore do not be foolish, but understand what the will of the Lord is.
Ephesians 5:17 (ESV)

Have you ever done something and then immediately thought, "Well that was foolish (or maybe you used the word stupid!)." We've all been there, and that usually happens when we don't take the time to think through the results or consequences of what we were doing. We just act without thinking, and it sometimes leads to something inevitable but undesirable as a result.

Young children often act foolishly. They haven't learned how gravity works and how things react when they are pulled and pushed on. We often see a young child doing something and immediately know what's about to happen even though the child is blissfully unaware of the impending danger. Why is this? Because the child lacks wisdom. They lack a lot of knowledge and the experience to know how to rightly apply that knowledge to the simple things they encounter in the world. They are learning, and they are quick learners!

As adults, we hope that we've grown in wisdom. In a worldly sense, most do. They grow to understand how gravity works and how things (and people!) react when they are pulled and pushed on. This is true in a worldly sense, but in a spiritual sense, it's not that simple. Apart from Christ, we are blinded by sin. We are dead in our trespasses and sin. There's no way that we can see and there's no way we can revive ourselves to escape the consequences and the cycle of sin in life. We're foolish when we're in the flesh.

However, as a believer, we've been made alive in Christ. We've been given sight to see the reality of what's true and what's false. We've been set free from sin and given the Spirit to empower us to obey. God's Word teaches us what is wise and true, and God's Word reveals to us what is foolish and false.

God's call for us in this verse is a continuation of the call to wisdom. It reinforces that call to be wise by commanding us to not be foolish! Don't return to childish ways and act foolishly in your life when it comes to sin. Rather, know what the will of the Lord is!

Many people make God's will out to be some great mystery that only a few can attain. There's nothing further from the truth. God's will has been clearly laid out for us in his Word. All we need for life and godliness is found in the revealed Will of God in Scripture (2 Peter 1:3). So knowing God's will is as simple as knowing God's Word, and being in God's will is as simple as desiring his will above anything else (Matthew 6:10). So surrender your life to God's will, and know his Word!

HEARING GOD'S WORD

Fill in the blanks below and discuss what God's Word means.

- **Therefore do not be _____ ,**

- **But _____ what the _____ of the Lord is.**

APPLYING GOD'S WORD

Look through the verse above, and answer these questions.

What is foolish behavior? How would you define "being foolish?"

What are the ways that you've acted foolishly as a believer? Be specific as you think about your life as a Christian. What's something that you've done recently that was foolish, and why was it foolish?

What does understanding the will of God have to do with not acting foolishly?

If surrendering your will to God's will and desiring his will is a key to knowing his will, are you surrendered to God's will in your life? Do you desire his will over anything else in your life?

How can the Lord's Prayer in Matthew 6 help you to seek God's will and grow in your surrender and desire for his will to be done?

RESPONDING TO GOD'S WORD

This week, respond to God's Word by not living foolishly and by knowing God's will...

(1) As you meditate on this verse throughout the week, ask the Lord to protect you by quickly identifying any foolish attitudes, thoughts, or actions in your life.
(2) Live wisely, trusting in the power of the Spirit to help you avoid foolish behavior.
(3) Seek God's will this week by surrendering your will to him! Take time to pray the Lord's Prayer every day – as much as needed – to focus your heart on truly desiring that his will would be done on earth as it is in heaven.
(4) Do God's will by following what he says as you read his Word each day and by seeking what he has to say over any questions or concerns that enter your heart this week.

LIVING GOD'S WORD

Put on the new life . . .

Did you do or say anything foolish? If so, make a note of that so that you can share with your group and ask for their prayers for your continued protection and growth in Christ.

If the Lord protected you from foolishness this week, praise him and worship him for his goodness and mercy! What a wonderful reminder of the presence and power of the Lord in our lives that's working for our good and his glory!

As you sought God's will this week, record the things that he revealed to you from his Word that are clearly things that are his will for your life. Thank him for his clarity and his truth that gives us direction and life.

PRAYING GOD'S WORD

Father, protect me from foolishness and lead me in your will. Keep my heart submitted to your will for my life, and fill my mind and my desires with your will as revealed in your Word!

LESSON 24

NEW LIFE: Living Sober

And do not get drunk with wine, for that is debauchery, but be filled with the Spirit….
Ephesians 5:18 (ESV)

Prisons are full of people who were filled with and then destroyed by a life that was devoted to some substance. Alcohol – and its modern twin of drugs – are substances that are often abused for selfish gain and escape.

The same substance that Jesus took on the night of his betrayal and used to memorialize his blood that would be shed for sin, is a substance that many take in excess to gain a euphoric feeling and to escape the realities of everyday life. Alcohol used in excess for the purpose of drunkenness is sin. The Lord called it debauchery, which is a word that carries the notion of abandoning moral restraint.

If you spend any time working with inmates, you'll see the stark and clear reality that this is a great definition of alcohol and drug abuse. Many are in prison because of something they did (murder, theft, etc.) that was driven by or at least influenced by their state-of-mind when they were abusing alcohol, drugs, or both. But you don't have to go to prison to see this reality, do you?

In every bar around town and in homes unknown behind closed doors, the evidence is there. Drunkenness and drug abuse lead to debauchery. These things give the flesh control, and the result is always the result of the flesh: Sin kills, steals, and destroys.

The antidote is clear and simple: The Spirit! The Lord didn't lay out a 12 step program that will bring freedom. He didn't say that this program or that program was the solution. Instead, he said that the answer was to be filled with the Spirit.

That answer is important to consider. The word "fill" means to completely fill up or to render full. In other words, the answer to victory of the flesh isn't more effort in the flesh, but it's that the flesh would be overwhelmed and pushed out by the Spirit. The solution is a life that's filled up completely with the Spirit so that there's no room left for sin.

This is both simple and supernatural. It's easy to understand, but it's impossible to accomplish apart from the miracle of God's grace and work in a believer's life. It also points to a mystery, which is that a believer receives the Holy Spirit in his/her new life in Christ, but the believer continually needs to be filled more-and-more with the Holy Spirit. This is the crucifixion and resurrection applied to your life (Galatians 5:24-25)! Be filled with the Spirit!

HEARING GOD'S WORD

Fill in the blanks below and discuss what God's Word means.

- **And do not get _____ with _____,**

- **For that is _____,**

- **But be _____ with the _____. . .**

APPLYING GOD'S WORD

Look through the verse above, and answer these questions.

Have you ever been drunk or high? When, and why? Was this a unique event or was it something you struggled with in your life before Christ or even after your salvation?

If you answered "yes" to the question above, did you ever find yourself in debauchery (abandoning your morals and inhibitions)? Why do you think this is such a common experience to those who are inebriated?

What does it mean to be filled with the Spirit? For a believer, who already has the Spirit in their life, how does this "filling" continue to happen? What are some keys to the filling of the Spirit as well as the quenching of the Spirit in a believer's life?

RESPONDING TO GOD'S WORD

This week, take time to respond to God's Word in these key ways:

(1) Are you abusing alcohol or drugs? If so, confess that to your group, and repent.

(2) How is drunkenness idolatry? Why is it important to see drug and alcohol abuse as sin rather than as a sickness? Which view is the view through God's Word? Which is the view through the modern eye of materialistic science?

(3) Do you know someone who is abusing alcohol or drugs? Pray for them, and find a way this week to share this lesson with them, pointing to the hope and the freedom that's only available in Christ.

(4) Ask for the Lord to fill you with the Spirit, and at the same time, ask him to crucify the flesh that's still taking up room in your heart.

LIVING GOD'S WORD

Put on the new life . . .

As you go through your week and encounter others who struggle with drug or alcohol abuse, make a list with their names so that you can remember to pray for them.

If you once abused alcohol or drugs and the Lord has changed that in your life, don't take that for granted. Write down your testimony in preparation of being able to share that with someone who is trapped in the sin of substance abuse.

As you prayed for the Lord to fill you in the Spirit, what specific ways did he answer that prayer this week. How did you see the evidence of the Spirit's presence and power at work in your life?

PRAYING GOD'S WORD

Lord, protect me from giving control of my life – my mind and my heart – to anything other than you. For those who are in bondage to sin and who have given themselves to drugs and alcohol, use me to point them to victory and to freedom in Jesus. Fill me with the Spirit so that my life will glorify you and will lead others to you.

LESSON 25

NEW LIFE: Living in a Community of Faith

Addressing one another in psalms and hymns and spiritual songs, singing and making melody to the Lord with your heart, 20 giving thanks always and for everything to God the Father in the name of our Lord Jesus Christ....
Ephesians 5:19-20 (ESV)

When was the last time you sang to someone else? Some have beautiful voices (or think they do!), and they often sing to others formally or informally, such as at church or to their spouse or children in their home. Others don't sing but in a crowd or in the privacy of their vehicle, but God actually calls us and expects us to address one another in song!

So here's the question again: What was the last time you sang to someone else? The answer to that question should be this past Sunday, when you gathered together to worship as the church and lifted your voices to the Lord. Did you realize that you weren't just singing to the Lord, but your singing was meant to be an encouragement to those around? When you sing to the Lord, you aren't just addressing God, but you're addressing your family, your friends, and your church around you in the hope and the joy of the Lord.

And true worship in song isn't just singing with our mouths, but it's singing from our hearts. As we sing Psalms, hymns, and spiritual songs, we should sing from our hearts, allowing the thanksgiving and praise and worship that's in our hearts to flow out of our mouths as we proclaim the truth about God and what he's done for us in Christ. This is worship in song, filled with thanksgiving for everything the Lord has done.

This verse also reminds us that there's no room for intolerance for different types of songs. Some people want only hymns. Others want only contemporary praise songs. The Lord in his wisdom demands that we sing different types of songs to him, including (1) the songs of Scripture that he himself wrote and gave to us to sing back to him; (2) hymns that are grounded in Scripture and written to be sung by all as the church gathers for worship; and (3) spiritual songs, which capture just about everything else! Why? There's something for everyone in this mix of praise in song, because we don't just sing to the Lord – the recipient of our praise – but we address one another as we sing to him!

To be clear, the only way to obey the Lord's direction in this verse is to participate in the worship of the Lord with his church, and in participating in worship, the only way to address one another in song is to sing! Make a joyful noise to the Lord. He deserves it. You need it, and others around you need you to show it and to share it.

HEARING GOD'S WORD

Fill in the blanks below and discuss what God's Word means.

- **Addressing one another in _____ and _____ and _____ songs,**

- **_____ and making _____ to the Lord with your heart,**

- **Giving _____ always and for _____**

- **To God the Father in the _____ of our Lord Jesus Christ.**

APPLYING GOD'S WORD

Look through the verse above, and answer these questions.

New Life in Christ is a life of praising and worshiping the Lord for all that he's given us in Christ. What did you learn about the importance of singing when the church gathers for worship? Is this new information to you, or is it something that you've always known?

If you are addressing people around you when you sing to the Lord in worship, what are you telling them? What do your words (spoken (sung) and unspoken (body language)) communicate to others? Is it a message of worship from your heart and thanksgiving from your soul?

What does thanksgiving look like in your heart? Are you giving thanks always and for everything?

RESPONDING TO GOD'S WORD

This week, respond to God's Word!

(1) Go to church! This is key to obedience to God's desire in how we address one another in song. You have to be with God's people in worship. Hopefully, this is a regular commitment and priority in your life. If not, make that commitment this week.

(2) Sing! You can't address those around you in psalms, hymns, and spiritual songs unless you sing. God didn't say that it must be on pitch or sound good. He said it needed to come from your heart. A heart that's full of worship and thanksgiving is a heart that overflows with praise. The more thankful you are to the Lord, the more you'll desire to sing to him!

(3) Address others as you sing! This isn't about singing in someone's face, but it is about recognizing the fact that you're singing is meant for others. Consider your family that's around you. Think about your brothers and sisters in Christ sitting where they can see you. Your worship is a communication to them. It's meant to encourage them in worship and reveal to them your thankfulness and praise to the Lord.

(4) Give thanks! Give thanks this week to the Lord for *everything*!

LIVING GOD'S WORD

Put on the new life . . .

Reflect on your commitment to corporate worship. Did it change in a positive way this week? Perhaps in a new or renewed way, was your commitment to join with your church in worship encouraged? Be prepared to share that change with your group.

As you sang to the Lord this week, how did you change the way you worshiped in singing as you recognized that your singing is intended to encourage others? How did the singing of others around you encourage you (or discourage you) this week?

What were the things that you gave thanks for this week? How did looking at *everything* for the purpose of giving thanks impact thankfulness in your heart?

PRAYING GOD'S WORD

Lord, grow my heart to sing to you. Use my singing to encourage others to praise you. Lead my soul to thank you for everything in the name of our Lord Jesus Christ!

LESSON 26

NEW LIFE: Living for Christ

Submitting to one another out of reverence for Christ.
Ephesians 5:21 (ESV)

An argument erupted in the deacon's meeting. The two men involved spoke to each other in tones that became increasingly loader and intimidatingly coarser. If it was a high-school argument, the circle would have already formed around them, with eyeballs waiting in anticipation for the first punch to be thrown.

What was the problem? Surely, it was a major issue of doctrinal compromise. Without a doubt, it must have been an incredibly crushing moral failure. Perhaps it was even a misunderstanding on an issue of ethics in the management of ministry.

Unfortunately, none of these was the issue that led to the fight of words. Rather, it was the thermostats. Someone was changing the thermostats in the church. With reckless abandon, they were taking it upon themselves to adjust the temperature settings on Sundays and Wednesday nights. One of the men was blaming the other for making the adjustments, and the pride of the two escalated an issue like that into an argument that altered the relationship and compromised their witness.

Why do things like this happen? The simple answer is sin. When we operate in the flesh rather than in the Spirit, sin wins. Pride rose up, and compromise and respect were defeated. So here's the command of the Lord: Submit to one another out of reverence for Christ!

Submission is something that most North Americans don't like. Independence and pride are built into the American mindset. From the roots of the pioneers who settled the land and fought for its freedoms, we don't like submission. But submission is something that God calls his people to do. Submitting to him requires submission in our relationships according to his design for submission in our lives, and for believers, the message is clear: Submit to one another out of reverence for Christ. In other words, in order to protect and to promote the glory of Christ in the church, submit to each other.

Of course, that submission is always perfectly faithful to God's Word. We aren't called to submit in ways that would lead to disobedience and unfaithfulness, but we are called to submit in ways that maintain and grow unity in Christ in the church.

Those deacons needed some submission, but they aren't the only ones. We all find ourselves in that place where pride rises up and arguments are just a word away. In those times, for the Lord's glory and when it doesn't lead to sin, submit to one another out of reverence for Christ.

80

HEARING GOD'S WORD

Fill in the blanks below and discuss what God's Word means.

- _____ to one _____

- Out of _____ for _____.

APPLYING GOD'S WORD

Look through the verse above, and answer these questions.

Use blueletterbible.org to look up the meaning of the word "submitting" in Ephesians 5:21. Write down a definition for submitting, and discuss what this word means.

When God said "to one another," who was he talking about? Who are believers to submit to when it comes to this command in our lives?

Again, use blueletterbible.org to look up the word reverence. Write down a definition for this word, and then discuss what it means. How does reverence in this case apply to Christ?

How does it show Christ reverence when believers submit to one another in a biblical way? How does it dishonor Christ when believers fail to submit to one another appropriately?

RESPONDING TO GOD'S WORD

This week, in every interaction you have with other believers, ask the Lord to show you what submission out of reverence for Christ means. If you feel pride rising in your heart or the desire to just be right in a matter that's disputable (Not a matter of compromise on doctrine or obedience), practice submission. Out of reverence for Christ, simply submit to the other believer, leaving the results in God's hands. You may be surprised at how the Lord uses that to accomplish his work in your lives and through your lives.

Put on the new life . . .

(1) Was submission to one another tested this week in your heart? If so, make a note of that by journaling about the experience and what you felt in your heart.

(2) If you were tempted this week not to submit, did you give in to temptation, or did you step in faith? Make a note in your journal about that experience so that you can share it with your group.

(3) If you did step in faith and submit to someone out of reverence for Christ, how did the Lord use that step of obedience? What happened, and what was the result that you immediately saw in the situation or relationship?

PRAYING GOD'S WORD

Father, it's hard to submit, but you've given us all we need in Christ, who submitted perfectly to your will, even to the point of death. In Christ, give me a heart of submission to others out of reverence for Christ. Help me to display even in my submission a great faith in you, which will encourage others to trust you. And Lord, help me do it all out of reverence for Christ. May my new life in him continue to grow to glorify him in every way, every day!

NEW LIFE NEXT

WHAT NOW?

The pursuit of growing in your new life in Jesus Christ never ends in this life. The apostle Paul reminds us of this reality in Philippians 3:12-14:

> *12 Not that I have already obtained this or am already perfect, but I press on to make it my own, because Christ Jesus has made me his own. 13 Brothers, I do not consider that I have made it my own. But one thing I do: forgetting what lies behind and straining forward to what lies ahead, 14 I press on toward the goal for the prize of the upward call of God in Christ Jesus* (Philippians 3:12-14, ESV).

So the new life journey never ends, and we hope you make it your aim to press on to make it your own, because Christ Jesus has made you his own!

The format of the New Life discipleship group is nothing new, and we hope it will never become something that's old. Our hope is that if you're new to small group discipleship, you'll continue to be involved in a discipleship group. If you're an old hand at small group discipleship, we pray that you'll keep your hand to the plow in the work of making disciples.

We also pray that New Life has taught or reinforced the basics of studying and applying God's Word such that you can now take any passage of Scripture, and in community with a small group of believers, you can work through that Scripture, identifying what it says, what it means, how it applies, and how to respond to it. We pray that you'll continue to be discipled, and as God grows you and prepares you, that you'll step into the role of the discipler, perhaps even using New Life to lead others to grow in their new life that's only possible in Jesus Christ.

NEW LIFE BIBLE READING PLAN

THE NEW TESTAMENT IN 52 WEEKS

Week 1
☐ Matthew 1
☐ Matthew 2
☐ Matthew 3
☐ Matthew 4
☐ Matthew 5

Week 2
☐ Matthew 6
☐ Matthew 7
☐ Matthew 8
☐ Matthew 9
☐ Matthew 10

Week 3
☐ Matthew 11
☐ Matthew 12
☐ Matthew 13
☐ Matthew 14
☐ Matthew 15

Week 4
☐ Matthew 16
☐ Matthew 17
☐ Matthew 18
☐ Matthew 19
☐ Matthew 20

Week 5
☐ Matthew 21
☐ Matthew 22
☐ Matthew 23
☐ Matthew 24
☐ Matthew 25

Week 6
☐ Matthew 26
☐ Matthew 27
☐ Matthew 28
☐ Mark 1
☐ Mark 2

Week 7
☐ Mark 3
☐ Mark 4
☐ Mark 5
☐ Mark 6
☐ Mark 7

Week 8
☐ Mark 8
☐ Mark 9
☐ Mark 10
☐ Mark 11
☐ Mark 12

Week 9
☐ Mark 13
☐ Mark 14
☐ Mark 15
☐ Mark 16
☐ Luke 1

Week 10
☐ Luke 2
☐ Luke 3
☐ Luke 4
☐ Luke 5
☐ Luke 6

Week 11
☐ Luke 7
☐ Luke 8
☐ Luke 9
☐ Luke 10
☐ Luke 11

Week 12
☐ Luke 12
☐ Luke 13
☐ Luke 14
☐ Luke 15
☐ Luke 16

Week 13
☐ Luke 17
☐ Luke 18
☐ Luke 19
☐ Luke 20
☐ Luke 21

Week 14
☐ Luke 22
☐ Luke 23
☐ Luke 24
☐ John 1
☐ John 2

Week 15
☐ John 3
☐ John 4
☐ John 5
☐ John 6
☐ John 7

Week 16
☐ John 8
☐ John 9
☐ John 10
☐ John 11
☐ John 12

Week 17
☐ John 13
☐ John 14
☐ John 15
☐ John 16
☐ John 17

Week 18
☐ John 18
☐ John 19
☐ John 20
☐ John 21
☐ Acts 1

Week 19
☐ Acts 2
☐ Acts 3
☐ Acts 4
☐ Acts 5
☐ Acts 6

Week 20
☐ Acts 7
☐ Acts 8
☐ Acts 9
☐ Acts 10
☐ Acts 11

Week 21
☐ Acts 12
☐ Acts 13
☐ Acts 14
☐ Acts 15
☐ Acts 16

Week 22
☐ Acts 17
☐ Acts 18
☐ Acts 19
☐ Acts 20
☐ Acts 21

Week 23
☐ Acts 22
☐ Acts 23
☐ Acts 24
☐ Acts 25
☐ Acts 26

Week 24
☐ Acts 27
☐ Acts 28
☐ Romans 1
☐ Romans 2
☐ Romans 3

Week 25
☐ Romans 4
☐ Romans 5
☐ Romans 6
☐ Romans 7
☐ Romans 8

Week 26
☐ Romans 9
☐ Romans 10
☐ Romans 11
☐ Romans 12
☐ Romans 13

Week 27
☐ Romans 14
☐ Romans 15
☐ Romans 16
☐ 1 Corinthians 1
☐ 1 Corinthians 2

Week 28
☐ 1 Corinthians 3
☐ 1 Corinthians 4
☐ 1 Corinthians 5
☐ 1 Corinthians 6
☐ 1 Corinthians 7

Week 29
- ☐ 1 Corinthians 8
- ☐ 1 Corinthians 9
- ☐ 1 Corinthians 10
- ☐ 1 Corinthians 11
- ☐ 1 Corinthians 12

Week 30
- ☐ 1 Corinthians 13
- ☐ 1 Corinthians 14
- ☐ 1 Corinthians 15
- ☐ 1 Corinthians 16
- ☐ 2 Corinthians 1

Week 31
- ☐ 2 Corinthians 2
- ☐ 2 Corinthians 3
- ☐ 2 Corinthians 4
- ☐ 2 Corinthians 5
- ☐ 2 Corinthians 6

Week 32
- ☐ 2 Corinthians 7
- ☐ 2 Corinthians 8
- ☐ 2 Corinthians 9
- ☐ 2 Corinthians 10
- ☐ 2 Corinthians 11

Week 33
- ☐ 2 Corinthians 12
- ☐ 2 Corinthians 13
- ☐ Galatians 1
- ☐ Galatians 2
- ☐ Galatians 3

Week 34
- ☐ Galatians 4
- ☐ Galatians 5
- ☐ Galatians 6
- ☐ Ephesians 1
- ☐ Ephesians 2

Week 35
- ☐ Ephesians 3
- ☐ Ephesians 4
- ☐ Ephesians 5
- ☐ Ephesians 6
- ☐ Philippians 1

Week 36
- ☐ Philippians 2
- ☐ Philippians 3
- ☐ Philippians 4
- ☐ Colossians 1
- ☐ Colossians 2

Week 37
- ☐ Colossians 3
- ☐ Colossians 4
- ☐ 1 Thessalonians 1
- ☐ 1 Thessalonians 2
- ☐ 1 Thessalonians 3

Week 38
- ☐ 1 Thessalonians 4
- ☐ 1 Thessalonians 5
- ☐ 2 Thessalonians 1
- ☐ 2 Thessalonians 2
- ☐ 2 Thessalonians 3

Week 39
- ☐ 1 Timothy 1
- ☐ 1 Timothy 2
- ☐ 1 Timothy 3
- ☐ 1 Timothy 4
- ☐ 1 Timothy 5

Week 40
- ☐ 1 Timothy 6
- ☐ 2 Timothy 1
- ☐ 2 Timothy 2
- ☐ 2 Timothy 3
- ☐ 2 Timothy 4

Week 41
- ☐ Titus 1
- ☐ Titus 2
- ☐ Titus 3
- ☐ Philemon 1
- ☐ Hebrews 1

Week 42
- ☐ Hebrews 2
- ☐ Hebrews 3
- ☐ Hebrews 4
- ☐ Hebrews 5
- ☐ Hebrews 6

Week 43
- ☐ Hebrews 7
- ☐ Hebrews 8
- ☐ Hebrews 9
- ☐ Hebrews 10
- ☐ Hebrews 11

Week 44
- ☐ Hebrews 12
- ☐ Hebrews 13
- ☐ James 1
- ☐ James 2
- ☐ James 3

Week 45
- ☐ James 4
- ☐ James 5
- ☐ 1 Peter 1
- ☐ 1 Peter 2
- ☐ 1 Peter 3

Week 46
- ☐ 1 Peter 4
- ☐ 1 Peter 5
- ☐ 2 Peter 1
- ☐ 2 Peter 2
- ☐ 2 Peter 3

Week 47
- ☐ 1 John 1
- ☐ 1 John 2
- ☐ 1 John 3
- ☐ 1 John 4
- ☐ 1 John 5

Week 48
- ☐ 2 John 1
- ☐ 3 John 1
- ☐ Jude 1
- ☐ Revelation 1
- ☐ Revelation 2

Week 49
- ☐ Revelation 3
- ☐ Revelation 4
- ☐ Revelation 5
- ☐ Revelation 6
- ☐ Revelation 7

Week 50
- ☐ Revelation 8
- ☐ Revelation 9
- ☐ Revelation 10
- ☐ Revelation 11
- ☐ Revelation 12

Week 51
- ☐ Revelation 13
- ☐ Revelation 14
- ☐ Revelation 15
- ☐ Revelation 16
- ☐ Revelation 17

Week 52
- ☐ Revelation 18
- ☐ Revelation 19
- ☐ Revelation 20
- ☐ Revelation 21
- ☐ Revelation 22

Parson's Porch Books

New Life: Growing in New Life that's only Possible in Jesus Christ
ISBN: Softcover 978-1-960326-06-5
Copyright © 2023 by Joel Williams

Parson's Porch Books is an imprint of Parson's Porch & Company (PP&C) in Cleveland, Tennessee. PP&C is a self-funded charity which earns money by publishing books of noted authors, representing all genres. Its face and voice is **David Russell Tullock** who you can contact at: dtullock@parsonsporch.com.

Parson's Porch & Company *turns books into bread & milk* by sharing its profits with the poor.

www.parsonsporch.com